SELLING SHORT

SELLING SHORT

RISKS, REWARDS, AND STRATEGIES FOR SHORT SELLING STOCKS, OPTIONS, AND FUTURES

Joseph A. Walker

JOHN WILEY & SONS, INC.

New York   Chichester   Brisbane   Toronto   Singapore

By the same author: *How the Options Markets Work*

Recognizing the importance of preserving what has been written, it is a policy of John Wiley & Sons, Inc., to have books of enduring value printed on acid-free paper, and we exert our best efforts to that end.

This publication is designed to provide accurate and authoritative information in regard to the subject matter covered. It is sold with the understanding that the publisher is not engaged in rendering legal, accounting, or other professional service. If legal advice or other expert assistance is required, the services of a competent professional person should be sought. *From a Declaration of Principles jointly adopted by a Committee of the American Bar Association and a Committee of Publishers.*

Library of Congress Cataloging-in-Publication Data

Walker, Joseph A.
    Selling short : risks, rewards, and strategies for short selling stocks, options, and futures / Joseph A. Walker.
      p.   cm. — (Wiley finance editions)
    Includes bibliographical references and index.
    ISBN 0-471-53464-1 (cloth)
    1. Short selling.   2. Speculation.   3. Securities.   4. Stocks.
    5. Options (Finance) 6. Commodity futures. I. Title. II. Series.
HG6041.W33 1991
332.63'228 — dc20   90-24800

Printed in the United States of America

10 9 8 7 6 5 4 3 2 1

You'll see . . . nothing will escape the bear market. I bet that within a week a five-franc piece will be worth no more than thirty centimes. Remember, I told you so, Mr. Coquardeau! (Drawing by Honoré Daumier. From the Arnhold and S. Bleichroeder, Inc., Collection. Reproduced by permission.)

Acknowledgments

The author wishes to acknowledge some of the friends who contributed their professional expertise to the preparation of this book.

Much gratitude is expressed to Ronald Berardino, Edward S. Bradley, Michael T. Curley, Fred Dahl, David M. Darst, Fred Eichelberg, Allan Pessin, William Rini, Arlene Robbins, and in particular to my wife, Barbara L. Walker, for her invaluable advice and endless patience.

Contents

1. SELLING SHORT: AN INTRODUCTION   **1**

The Ethics of Selling Short   3
How Markets Benefit from Short Selling   5
The Historical Significance of Short Selling   7

2. A LOOK BACK: CORNERS AND BEAR RAIDS   **9**

Clarence Saunders and Piggly Wiggly Stores   11
Allan Ryan and Stutz Motor Car Company   15

3. THE REGULATORS ARRIVE   **21**

The Northern Pacific Bear Raid   21
Jay Gould and the Gold Corner   24
The Crash of 1929   25
The SEC is Born   27
Reforming the Exchanges   30

4. **THE LAWS, THE RULES, THE RESULTS**   **33**

The Plus Tick Rule 34
The Short Selling Transaction 34
Rumer Spreading and Insider Trading 38
Stock Parking 45

5. **APPLICATIONS OF SELLING SHORT**   **49**

Speculating by Selling Short 49
Other Uses of Short Selling 52

6. **THE MECHANICS OF SELLING SHORT**   **67**

The Margin Account 68
Rules for Purchasing Securities 68
The Short Selling Process 70
Rights and Obligations 76
Fees and Complications 79

7. **PROTECTING SHORT POSITIONS:
    EQUITY OPTIONS**   **83**

Stop Orders 83
Equity Options 86
Options as a Substitute for Selling Short 93
Straddles and Combinations 96
Options on Other Products 102

8. **DECISION MAKING THROUGH
    MARKET ANALYSIS**   **115**

The Random Walk Theory 116
The Hemline Hypothesis 117
The Super Bowl Theory 117
Fundamental Analysis 120
Technical Analysis 125
Chart Patterns 130

9. COMMODITY FUTURES   137

Short Selling Futures   140
Hedging with Futures   142
The Future of Futures   146

10. STOCK INDEX FUTURES AND PROGRAM TRADING   147

Index Futures and the Institutional Investor   149
Program Trading   152
Program Trading and Crashes   155
Portfolio Insurance   158
Circuit Breakers and Other Controls   159

11. BEWARE THE BEAR   163

Pity the Bear?   165
The Short Seller and the 1987 Crash   166
A Look Ahead   168

GLOSSARY   171

BIBLIOGRAPHY   187

INDEX   191

SELLING SHORT

1

Selling Short: An Introduction

short . . . less than or lacking a sufficient or correct amount.

Webster's New World Dictionary

How many times have you heard someone use the word *short* to express the meaning given above?

"I can't go on vacation this year as I'm short of money."

"I would have had a par on the third hole but the putt was short."

"I would have hired him but he's short on experience."

In financial markets, the word is used in much the same way: a *short sale* is the sale of a security that the seller does not own. Although there are many variations of selling short, all of which will be discussed, the usual purpose is to sell at today's price and purchase later at a lower price. It is simply the reverse of the normal procedure. Generally, an investor seeks out a security that she feels will increase in value. She purchases it, and if she is correct in her judgment she sells it later at a profit. But suppose her analysis led her to the conclusion that a particular stock was due for a decline in value? Should she be a bystander as the market drops? No. Here is the place for the short sale. Our client can sell now, and, when the decline occurs, she can purchase at the lower price.

For example, with IBM stock trading in the market at $105 a share, client A is convinced that the price will rise. He enters the following order:

Buy
  100   IBM   Market

Market means the best price available at the time. Client A purchases 100 shares of IBM stock at approximately $105 a share for a total cost of about $10,500. Some time later, IBM reports greatly improved earnings, and other investors rush in to purchase shares, driving the price up to $125 a share. Our happy client A now sells his shares at that price and receives $12,500. He has a profit of $2,000 less any commissions or other costs involved in making the transactions.

At the time client A is making his purchase, client B is also studying the prospects for IBM stock. She concludes that the immediate future is not very rosy. She does not own any IBM shares and therefore will suffer no loss if the price does in fact decline. If she wishes to act in a conservative manner, she will do nothing; she will wait until the price falls to a level she thinks attractive and then, perhaps, buy the stock. But client B wishes to take immediate advantage of her feeling that the price will fall. If she has the financial and emotional ability to take the risk, she may enter the following order:

Sell
  100   IBM   Market (Short)

As we will see later in our study, this order must be clearly marked as a *short* sale. If a person owns the shares being sold, the sale is called a *long* sale. Client B owns no IBM stock; she is selling short.

Her order is executed, and she sells the stock at $105 a share. But she does not own any shares; how does she deliver the IBM stock to the buyer? She borrows the stock from some other person who owns it. This process will also be discussed in detail in a later chapter. As client B foresaw, IBM's stock drops to a price of $90. She purchases at this price and pays about $9,000. (This is known as *covering the short*.) Since she sold at $10,500 ($105 a share) she has a *profit* of $1,500 less any transaction costs.

Both client A and client B did exactly the same thing. They purchased IBM stock at one price and sold it for a profit at a higher price. They made the two transactions in a different order, but the result was the same. It is important to point out, however, that there was one important difference between the actions of these two clients—the potential risk.

When client A purchased IBM stock for $10,500, his risk was limited. In the most unlikely circumstance that IBM would become worthless, he could lose no more than his purchase cost of $10,500.

Client B, on the other hand, has taken on an unlimited risk. At some future date, she must cover the short and repurchase the shares. The price she pays will be compared to the proceeds of her sale ($10,500) to determine her profit or loss. We cannot determine what price she will pay to purchase. IBM could rise to $200, $300, $500, or even $1,000 a share. How high is up? While there are ways in which client B can protect her position, she can still lose an indeterminable amount on the short sale.

For those able to afford this risk, selling short provides a technique for profiting in a declining market. In practice, however, very few investors are capable of such risks and most should generally avoid this practice. It is nonetheless important that all investors understand the technique, as it plays an integral part in securities markets.

THE ETHICS OF SELLING SHORT

There are some who feel that selling securities short is unethical. To sell something that you do not have may seem a deceptive practice. Yet similar practices are used in virtually every industry.

A short time ago, the newspapers carried a story about a major U.S. aircraft manufacturer concluding a contract to sell more than 100 jet planes to a foreign country. The details were set, the price determined, and the contract signed. Did the manufacturer have the planes in stock? Of course not. The company was selling the planes short. It would now begin to manufacture the aircraft and would deliver according to the agreed terms. At the time the sale was made, however, the company sold something it did not have.

The sports page might have a headline like this: "All-star first baseman Joe Muscles signs five-year contract for $20 million." Good news for Joe, but he has just sold five years of his services short. He has not, in fact cannot, deliver the "at bats" and home runs at the time he signs the contract. He may be able to in the future, but at the time he signed the contract, he made a short sale.

Have you or an associate ever set out to purchase a home in a new development? If so, you may have experienced the following scenario. You drove to the housing site and looked out over 150 acres of woods. At the entrance were three model homes: a split level, a colonial, and a Cape Cod. You chose the colonial. You then selected the building location you preferred, and the developer drove you out to see it: two beautiful acres of trees, weeds, and underbrush. But you still signed the contract and bought the house. What house? The developer sold the house short. He did not have it, but he agreed to deliver it on a future date.

Client B in the earlier example did nothing different from what the manufacturer, the baseball player, or the housing developer did. They each sold a product or a service short. They each agreed to deliver in the future. If they do make delivery properly, the result will be no different from what it would have been had they contracted to sell something they owned.

Perhaps short sellers can be compared to that persecuted minority, left-handed people. Left-handed people do the same things as right-handed people do; they just do them from the opposite direction. Short sellers are the left-handed people of the investment world.

Were it not for short selling, investing would be a one-way street. Markets rise and markets fall. If you could profit only when prices rose, you would be utilizing only half of the market's potential.

If the roads in your city ran only north, the town would soon be empty because no one could return. Markets, like roads, go in different directions to allow for convenient entrance and exit.

We will leave the judgment about the morality of short selling to others more competent in such areas. However, the fact that short selling improves the marketability of securities is beyond argument. The practice benefits the market at large and can improve investment results even for the vast majority of investors who never sell securities short.

HOW MARKETS BENEFIT FROM SHORT SELLING

Suppose you wish to purchase 100 shares of General Motors stock; further suppose that selling short is prohibited. You will place your order, perhaps on the floor of the New York Stock Exchange.

You will have to purchase the shares from someone who owns them and who is selling the shares long. Although the last sale was at 45⅝, the lowest current asking price is $46 a share. This is what you will have to pay. But if short selling *is* allowed, a shareholder who is anticipating a decline in General Motors stock might be willing to sell 100 shares short at $45¾ a share. By paying this lesser price, you save $0.25 a share, or $25 on the 100 shares. It makes no difference to you that the seller is shorting the stock; in fact, you will not even be told that he is. All that concerns you is that the seller deliver the stock. This he will do by borrowing the shares.

Suppose that a shareholder wishes to sell 100 shares of AT&T stock. She bought the stock some time ago at $20 a share, and the current price is about $42. She stands to make a nice profit. She enters the following order:

Sell   100   AT&T   Market (Long)

If short selling is prohibited, the shareholder might sell at $42 a share. But in a market where short selling is not prohibited, a buyer might make a bid of $42⅛ to cover a short sale he had made earlier. Our happy seller increases her profit by $12.50 ($0.125 a share). Again, it is of no concern to her that the buyer is a short seller. All that matters to her is that she is being paid ⅛ point more than she would have been otherwise.

In each of our examples, the non–short seller had his or her price improved due to the presence of a short seller. The increase in liquidity is good for all investors and for the market in general.

The basic point about short selling is this: The person short selling securities generally does so because he believes the market will decline. Later, whether he was right or wrong, he repurchases the security to cover the short. This adds volume to the trading and is generally beneficial to all.

While the anticipation of a falling market is the most common application of short selling, it is by no means the only one. The many varieties of short selling lead to other strategies that may be advantageous to an investor.

In addition to the simple short sale used in previous examples, there are other forms of the technique. The short sale can be used to advantage when a disparity in price is found between two markets. This practice is called *arbitrage* (from the French meaning "to judge"). As we will demonstrate later, the arbitrageur purchases a security in one market and simultaneously sells it, often short, in another market. An arbitrage can also consist of the purchase of one security, such as a convertible bond, and the simultaneous short sale of the security into which the bond is convertible. Arbitrage can also be used to profit from market differences arising during merger or tender offers. Some examples of arbitrage are risk-free and therefore quite difficult to uncover. Others, called *risk arbitrage*, are more speculative and can often lead to disastrous results.

While most short sales involve the sale of a security that the seller does not own, others arise when the seller owns the security but does not plan to deliver it. She will accomplish delivery in the same manner as in the more common short sales, by borrowing the stock. This form of short selling is called *short against the box* (or *short versus box*) and indicates that the seller has the shares in her safety deposit box, but plans to accomplish delivery by using borrowed shares. The short versus box method can be used to take advantage of temporary market declines and can be most useful in tax planning, as it permits a taxpayer to defer liability on a gain from the year of the sale to a later year.

We will also look at a kind of short sale known as *short exempt*. Short sales that qualify for this designation are exempt from some of the rules that apply to the other forms of the technique.

Short selling is a most useful and varied technique, but very little has been written about it as it is not everyone's cup of tea. While investors are accustomed to buying and selling, very few ever have or ever will execute a short sale. Therefore, the practice has acquired the reputation of being strange or mysterious. It is in fact no more strange or mysterious than your left-handed cousin, although in some cases this may not be an ideal analogy. We will study the process thoroughly. If you find short selling a concept that can help your investment program, then you will have made a new friend. If you find that the inherent dangers are too great for you, at least you will know your enemy.

THE HISTORICAL SIGNIFICANCE OF SHORT SELLING

Before proceeding with the uses and procedures of short selling, it is important to look back at some of the history of the device. In some instances that history is not a proud one, but it must be understood in order to appreciate the present. The use of short selling to implement market abuses in part led to major investigations and legislation by the federal government. An awareness of these events is an important factor in the education of the intelligent investor.

Short selling can probably be traced back to the Dark Ages, but it is the early years of the twentieth century that are the most critical to this subject.

2

A Look Back:
Corners and Bear Raids

Every person who has followed securities markets is familiar with the terms *bull* and *bear*. The bull anticipates a rising market, while the bear sees a declining market on the horizon. One legend tells us that the terms are derived from the method these animals employ in attacking their enemies. The bull will charge a foe and gore in an upward motion. The bear will humble his opposition by crushing him with a downward attack. This may not be true, but it does provide an interesting explanation. The fact is that bulls and bears do not always feel that the market may move in their particular direction; on the other hand, they are fearful that a detrimental trend may occur. In such cases, they may take precautionary measures to protect positions that may be adversely affected if their fears are realized.

In the history of securities trading, many instances have been recorded in which the bears not only anticipated a market decline but took direct steps to cause the decline to occur. They accomplished this through short selling the security, and the events were called *bear raids*.

For example, suppose that a group of speculators working to

gether wish to profit from the price decline of a stock. The group begins to sell the stock short at perhaps $90 a share. This selling depresses the price, and our manipulators continue to sell short at successively lower prices.

Their continued sales force the price down to 85 then to 80, 75 and 70. The public owners of the stock now panic and begin to sell their shares. Having started the snowball down the hill, the bear raiders cease selling and watch as the public sales force the price down to 60, then 50 and 40. At this point, the raiders buy the stock, covering the shorts made at higher prices with an excellent profit. In some cases, the raiders might be able to take control of a company at an artificially reduced price, enhancing their profit still further. Regulations enacted in more recent years have made bear raids legally impossible, but in the earlier part of the twentieth century, such manipulations were not unusual.

The counterattack to a bear raid is called a *corner*. Remember, a short seller must borrow the stock to make delivery to the purchaser. Suppose the short seller is unable to borrow the necessary shares. The purchaser can demand delivery, requiring the short seller to cover his short by purchasing the stock himself. This causes a rise in the price of the stock, defeating the bear raider's purpose.

The classic corner occurs when the principals of a company that is the subject of a bear raid become aware of the attack. They quietly purchase shares as the bear raiders sell, thus acquiring all or a large part of the outstanding stock. When they have cornered the market, they then demand delivery of the shares and when the bear raiders attempt to borrow the stock, they find it unavailable. The party with the corner refuses to lend the stock other than at a price far above the current market value. The bear raiders are defeated, and justice again triumphs. Life, however, is seldom a fairy tale in which the good guy always wins.

Two bear raids that occurred earlier in this century are worth our attention. One involved the Stutz Motor Car Company of America, and the other, a company called Piggly Wiggly Stores. In examining these two examples, you will see all the elements—bear raids, corners, manipulation, persecution, and greed—that marked this part of investment history. Neither story had a happy end-ing, but each taught important lessons that led to changes that improved later markets.

CLARENCE SAUNDERS AND PIGGLY WIGGLY STORES

During the closing years of the 1980s, a new kind of retail store, originally developed in France, was introduced in the United States. Given the name *hypermarkets,* these stores combined the product lines of supermarkets and department stores into one huge selling area. In sheer size, a hypermarket is to a supermarket what a basketball is to a baseball. One hypermarket in Philadelphia contains more than 300,000 square feet of selling space, which is just slightly smaller than the combined area of seven football fields. While the future success or failure of hypermarkets has not yet been determined, they surely represent a radical innovation in the retailing of consumer goods.

An event almost as futuristic in concept for its time occurred in Memphis, Tennessee, in 1919. A gentleman named Clarence Saunders began developing a chain of self-service grocery stores, forerunners of today's supermarkets. He gave the business the attention-attracting name of Piggly Wiggly Stores. The business grew rapidly, and within a few years there were more than 1,000 Piggly Wiggly stores doing business. More than half of these were owned by the company; the rest were franchised to independent owners. (The franchise was also a relatively unknown merchandising method in those years.)

The Virginia-born Saunders had all of the characteristics required for a Horatio Alger–like career. His family was far from wealthy, and he began his working life in the grocery business while still in his teens. He moved up from working as a store clerk to owning a wholesale business, and at one point owned a small group of stores that he later sold. Though his early career was successful, the most exciting chapters began with the establishment of Piggly Wiggly. Although not yet forty years of age, Saunders had acquired a deep experience in retailing and chose the right avenue in which to apply it. His personal life was not conducted in a quiet manner. Shortly after establishing his business in 1919, Saunders began construction of a massive mansion complete with his own private golf course. Built of pink Georgia marble, the structure quite naturally acquired the name the Pink Palace. While much of Saunders' private life was touched with flamboyance, his business decisions were those of a shrewd, calculating professional.

The true beginning of our story was in 1922 when Piggly Wiggly Stores applied to list its shares for trading on the New York Stock Exchange. Trading in the company's shares could be best described as sleepy. As with the stock of most food chains, Piggly Wiggly stock paid a reasonably attractive dividend and so would be best categorized as a conservative security. It could hardly have been viewed as a vehicle for one of the most sensational market episodes of the twentieth century.

The stock of Piggly Wiggly, of which only 200,000 shares were outstanding, was trading at about $50 a share when an event occurred that led to the downfall of many people. Some independently owned Piggly Wiggly stores in the Northeast failed and ceased doing business. Since these stores were not owned by the company, their ill fortune had little if any effect on the health of the enterprise. But some market operatives interpreted, or perhaps misinterpreted, the stores' failures as an indication that the entire company was on the brink of disaster. This was the ideal setting, they concluded, for a bear raid. These people, whose names were never made public, began short selling Piggly Wiggly stock. The price of the stock declined and brought the matter to Saunders' attention. He determined to fight the raiders and began purchasing the company's stock on the Exchange. Saunders viewed this struggle as a battle of good against evil, and to assist him in his quest he enlisted the services of some Wall Street professionals, among them the famous Jesse L. Livermore.

Livermore was one of Wall Street's best-known market speculators. During his career he played a part in some of the industry's most notorious speculations, with bear raids high on his list of triumphs. By enlisting Livermore's service, Saunders was simply applying the well-known principle that "it takes one to know one."

While Livermore's Wall Street life was replete with the drama of victory and defeat, his death was an example of expectations unfulfilled. Although Livermore continued to play a major part as a market speculator through the 1920s and 1930s, the good fortune that graced his early efforts began to elude him toward the end of his life. Having made and lost fortunes during his spectacular career, he finally found himself nearly penniless. He ended his problems in 1940, when he walked into the restroom in the Sherry-Netherland Hotel in New York City, drew out a pistol, and put a bullet through his head.

Saunders punctuated his campaign with advertisements in which he pictured himself as the knight with the golden sword doing battle against the dark forces of Satan. But his purchases continued, and in a short time he owned more than half the outstanding stock of Piggly Wiggly Stores. The price had risen above $60, and the bear raiders were becoming justifiably nervous. Saunders also had reason to be concerned: If he successfully cornered all of the shares and the short sellers were unable to deliver, where would he sell his holdings? Saunders developed a strategy that would inject stock into the floating supply without making it available to the bear raiders. He offered 50,000 shares to public investors at a price substantially below the then-current market price of about $70. The shares, however, could be purchased only on an installment-like plan and could not be physically delivered until the final payment was made. Therefore, the bear raiders could not borrow these shares to deliver against their short sales and Saunders could relieve himself of some of the debt he had taken on to wage his battle.

At about this time, Livermore disassociated himself from the Saunders team, leaving the man from Memphis to conclude the affair by himself. Saunders demanded delivery of the shares owed to him by the short sellers. Since he had by now successfully cornered all the stock, there was no one from whom they could borrow the stock except him. The few shares that remained in other hands were in ferocious demand, and Piggly Wiggly stock rose above $120 a share.

Then the ax fell. The New York Stock Exchange granted additional time beyond the usual one day for the short sellers to make delivery; it also suspended trading in Piggly Wiggly shares. Saunders demanded delivery of the shares, which he offered to sell at $150 a share. The price would rise above that level if the bears did not comply immediately. But again the NYSE acted against Saunders, this time by permanently delisting Piggly Wiggly shares and by granting additional time for the short sellers. Saunders was forced to drop his settlement price to $100; this, together with the acquisition of the few outstanding shares remaining, allowed the bears to settle their contracts. Although the bears suffered losses, Saunders was the real loser. He now owned virtually all of the company's stock, for which there was no market, and he was still burdened with the huge debt he had undertaken.

Did the Exchange act improperly to protect its members, some of whom were reputed to be among the bear raiders? We will never be certain, but some observers clearly saw this as the truth of the matter. Others, however, defended the Exchange's actions as necessary to protect the integrity and continuity of the marketplace. You must draw your own conclusion.

Despite the money received from the raiders, Saunders found himself many millions of dollars in debt. He attempted to enlist the support of the citizens of Memphis by offering 50,000 shares of Piggly Wiggly at $55 a share. As a show of good faith, he even boarded up the still-unfinished Pink Palace (later converted to a museum by the City of Memphis). But the effort failed when Saunders refused to permit an audit of the company's books. Soon thereafter, he began selling off some of the stores to raise the cash needed to meet maturing debts. But even this effort failed, and Saunders was forced to resign and turn over the company to his creditors. Although forced to declare bankruptcy, Saunders eventually acquired another, though smaller, fortune, with a new store chain. That chain, however, was also forced into bankruptcy during the early years of the depression of the 1930s.

Until his death in 1953 at the age of 71, Saunders kept coming up with ideas for advancing the art of retailing. He attempted to develop an automated grocery store, but the machinery and construction costs proved prohibitive. Although many of his ideas might be implemented quite easily today, unfortunately for him, Clarence Saunders lived in the precomputer age.

Who were the winners and losers in the bear raid and corner game over Piggly Wiggly? Both the short sellers and Saunders lost money, but the bear raiders survived to play another day. Though Saunders was twice forced into bankruptcy, his life-style was never greatly reduced, and he lived in a fairly opulent manner until the end of his life.

So perhaps the only real losers were the investors who lost money on the company's shares and who were not even playing the game. As for the bear raiders and Clarence Saunders, it would appear that their game ended in a tie.

ALLAN RYAN AND STUTZ MOTOR CAR COMPANY

The contestants in the Piggly Wiggly episode came from different worlds: On one side, Saunders, the poor-born Southern boy turned retailing entrepreneur, and on the other, the professional market traders of the Eastern financial establishment—as unlike as catfish and caviar. This was not the case in the bear raid on Stutz Motor Car Company of America. Both the bull, Allan A. Ryan, and most, if not in fact all, of the bears were members of the prestigious New York Stock Exchange. Despite this important difference, the tactics used in both contests were virtually identical, and the result again produced no real winner.

Unless you are a fan of old movies or automotive museums, it is not likely that you have seen a Stutz Bearcat. But in the early years of the horseless carriage, the Bearcat was the state-of-the-art vehicle. Although the company produced other models, the sporty Bearcat was the favorite of the youth of that era. Put on the raccoon coat and the straw boater, jump into the Bearcat, wave your banner, and head for the game (the Yale-Harvard game, of course).

In 1916, Allan A. Ryan became president of the Stutz Motor Car Company. Ryan was a member of the New York Stock Exchange and one of Wall Street's most aggressive bulls. He made investments in many companies in a variety of fields, and his reputation for aggressiveness usually resulted in other investors following his lead. This led to wave after wave of profits for Ryan, and well before his fortieth birthday he was a millionaire many times over.

Unlike Clarence Saunders, however, Allan Ryan had never tasted the acid of poverty, for he was the son of the transportation tycoon Thomas Fortune Ryan. The elder Ryan had begun to amass his wealth in 1880 by joining a group that eventually owned and controlled virtually the entire transportation system of the City of

New York. T. F. Ryan expanded his activities to other fields, and by the time the Roaring Twenties arrived, he was reputed to be one of the richest men in the United States. The Ryans, father and son, were later to have a falling out that lasted until T. F. Ryan's death in 1928. But in 1915, the elder Ryan presented his son with a seat on the New York Stock Exchange.

Allan A. Ryan was born in 1880, just as his father's fortune had begun to grow, but he had still been given all of the advantages reserved for the children of the wealthy. He attended private schools and Georgetown University (his father was a major contributor to the Catholic church), and he eventually made his way to his appointed destiny on Wall Street. By early 1920, Allan Ryan was a major force on the Exchange. His firm, Allan A. Ryan & Co., Inc., had built a power base by making large purchases of stock in growing American companies and profiting from their rise in price as the economy continued to improve. These profits were often gleaned at the expense of short sellers of these same stocks who were forced to cover their positions at successively higher prices. This may in fact have led to the events that were to occur shortly thereafter.

In the early part of 1920, Stutz stock experienced a dramatic increase in value and, in early February, rose above $130 a share. Such sharp movements were not unusual in those years, as the volume of trading was infinitesimal by today's standards. In fact, on February 2, 1920, when Stutz stock reached $134 a share, the total volume of trading for all stocks on the Exchange was 487,000 shares. In markets of today, a volume of 150 million shares in a day would be considered average or perhaps even a bit slow.

In the years of the bear raids on Piggly Wiggly and Stutz, companies with only 200,000 shares or even less could be traded on the Exchange. Today, a company must have more than 1 million outstanding shares before it can even be considered for listing. Most companies have many times that amount. The scarcity of shares in the 1920s allowed for more startling price gyrations.

As the price of Stutz stock rose, Ryan became aware that a group of short sellers, many of them members of the NYSE, had banded together to conduct a bear raid on the company. Feeling the price to be too high, they wished to force it down through the weight of their short sales and turn a handsome profit. Ryan, however, would prove to be a formidable opponent. Given his prior history, it is possible that he welcomed the opportunity to wage the war. While the early Christians had entered the arena to fight lions and had lost, Ryan had made a fortune by winning battles with bears.

Ryan began to purchase Stutz stock with an eye toward cornering the market and bringing the bears to their knees. Although the price declined a bit initially, the power of Ryan's buying campaign eventually reversed the direction of the trend, and by April 1920 the price of Stutz stock neared $400 a share. Many Stutz investors, not themselves involved in the contest, happily sold their shares at nice profits. Ryan bought these shares. As the price rose, the bear raiders became more convinced that the price must fall, and they continued to sell short. Ryan bought these shares as well. At first Ryan accommodated the short sellers by lending them stock to allow them to make delivery. But this was part of the game: Don't pull up the net until all the fish are trapped. By lending stock, Ryan was also able to ascertain the identity of the short sellers. He felt such knowledge might be useful in the future. Ryan accomplished his corner; he and his associates owned all of the shares of Stutz Motor Car Company. He would demand delivery, which would require the short sellers to borrow the shares. The only source from which they could borrow was Allan Ryan. Would he lend stock to those who had hoped to destroy him and his company? Of course he would. But only at a price that he would set. That price was $750 a share.

At this point, the Stutz story takes a turn similar to that of Piggly Wiggly Stores. Although the players on both sides were members of the New York Stock Exchange, the Exchange acted in a manner that could benefit only one side—the bear raiders.

Ryan was called to appear before the Exchange's Conduct Committee to discuss the unusual situation in the trading of Stutz. Ryan stated his position and repeated his offer to settle all outstanding contracts at $750 a share. This was in complete accord with existing Exchange rules, which required that sellers deliver shares in accordance with the terms of their contracts. If forced to borrow the shares, they would be required to settle on whatever terms were available, and in this case, the terms were to be dictated by Allan

Ryan. The Exchange intervened to protect the short sellers. Later that same day, they informed Ryan that they would remove Stutz shares from trading due to a lack of available supply. Although this would severely damage Ryan's ability to trade in the shares, he did not back down. Instead, he threatened to raise his price to $1,000 a share if the Exchange carried out its threat. The New York Stock Exchange members, however, felt that they were bound by no rules, either written or implied. At the close of business on March 31, 1920, the shares of Stutz Motor Car were suspended from trading by the Governing Committee of the Exchange. A few days later the committee went even further, stating that the Exchange would not consider the short sellers' failure to deliver Stutz shares to be a breach of contract. Ryan resigned his membership in a blistering notice that questioned both the motives and the morals of the staid New York Stock Exchange. His departure also removed him from the jurisdiction of that august body and freed him to continue his fight. Ryan released to the press the names of a number of Exchange members who owed him Stutz stock. This constituted an indictment of them as members of the bear-raiding group.

Eventually a committee was agreed upon to negotiate a settlement price for the undelivered shares. With Ryan continuing to threaten to sell back the shares at his price, the committee proposed a settlement price of $550 a share. While this price was well below his earlier demands, Ryan, deep in debt to finance his corner, accepted the offer without hesitation.

At this point, it appeared that the Stutz matter had ended; that was not at all the case. As with Clarence Saunders and Piggly Wiggly, Ryan's profits were not nearly sufficient to pay his accumulated debts. Though he now owned all Stutz stock, it had no ready market, as it was still denied listing on the Exchange. To make matters worse, the Exchange, ignoring Ryan's earlier resignation, eventually expelled him from membership, citing his violations of "just and equitable principles of trade."

The banks continued to press Ryan for payment, but since his major asset consisted of the unmarketable Stutz shares, he was unable to meet their demands. In July 1922, he declared bankruptcy, listing liabilities in excess of $30 million. His Stutz stock was sold at auction for $20 a share, dramatically below the price of $750 a share he had demanded from the short sellers only two years earlier.

Allan A. Ryan never again became a factor in financial circles. Although he actively attempted to reconstruct his empire, he never succeeded. He died in 1940.

Two years earlier the Stutz Motor Car Company itself had died. It had never duplicated its early success, and the difficult depression years sealed its doom.

Allan Ryan won the battle but ended up bankrupt. The bear raiders may have suffered severe financial losses, but as far as can be determined, they remained in business to deal another day.

If any good came of the bear raids, it was the part they unintentionally played in furthering the enactment of the federal laws and industry regulations that prevented repetition of this type of action. This is not to say that manipulative and unethical practices did not continue, but the Piggly Wiggly and Stutz Motor Car bear raids and other similar events awakened the public and the financial community to the need for effective and enforceable controls.

Although it may seem impossible, there were no effective federal securities laws in the United States until 1933. For the entire period of the 1920s until well into the depression, the markets were conducted without externally composed standards or requirements. This was soon to change.

3
The Regulators Arrive

The bear raids described in Chapter 2 were not the only events that led to the historic changes in the securities industry in the 1930s. In fact, the Piggly Wiggly Stores and Stutz Motor Car Company bear raids were somewhat isolated situations that for the most part affected only the parties involved.

In contrast, the market crash of 1929 shook the financial foundation of the American economy. The bank failures and unemployment that followed led to a nationwide depression that was ended only by the onset of World War II. In fact, the Piggly Wiggly and Stutz bear raids were only minor occurrences when compared with a much earlier bear raid on Northern Pacific Railroad. This piece of financial history involved many of the great names in business and commerce and dealt a severe blow to public confidence in securities markets. It was to provide a lesson that would often be cited as a reason for the regulation that surfaced more than thirty years later.

THE NORTHERN PACIFIC BEAR RAID

In early 1901, two powerful but widely disparate groups sought to gain control of the Burlington Railroad. The Burlington, whose proper name was the Chicago, Burlington & Quincy Railroad, was a relatively small line, but it held a great attraction for its two suitors. One group was led by James J. Hill, who controlled the much larger Northern Pacific Railroad. Hill desired control over the Burlington to prevent it from increasing its competition in the Northern Pacific's exclusive territory. The acquisition would also provide the Northern Pacific with access to the Chicago market, which was then, as now, the main center of the transportation network in the United States.

The second group was headed by E. H. Harriman, the head of the Union Pacific Railroad. The Burlington's routes paralleled many of Union Pacific's routes, and Harriman feared that Union Pacific's ability to compete would be greatly enhanced if the Burlington were controlled by stronger hands.

As different as were the major players—Hill and Harriman— perhaps even more diverse were the bankers they chose to represent them. Hill employed the services of J. P. Morgan & Company and its legendary leader, J. P. Morgan himself. The house of Morgan had long been the leading factor in the financing of American industry. Its name and reputation were the epitome of the stereotype of the Protestant Yankee banker who controlled most of the industry.

Harriman, on the other hand, chose as his ally the firm of Kuhn Loeb & Co., a firm that would be a leader in finance for many decades to come. Kuhn Loeb, however, was headed by a gentleman named Jacob Schiff. While an admitted genius in financial matters, Schiff was an immigrant Jew who was not totally accepted by his investment-banking peers. Although Schiff's accomplishments would lead to positive change, at this period in 1901, those events still lay in the future.

Both groups began buying Burlington shares in the open market, but the Hill-Morgan team also negotiated privately with large holders of the stock and made purchases at prices as high as $200 a share. In time they gained control and appeared to have won the battle of the Burlington Railroad. The Harriman-Schiff team, however, would not surrender. If they could not own the Burlington, then they would buy control of the Northern Pacific and own the entire system, the Burlington included.

In a buying spree unprecedented in those days, Harriman purchased a majority of Northern Pacific shares in a period of just a few months. Hill and Morgan purchased as well, and Northern Pacific's price rose to more than $150 a share. Although Harriman owned a majority of common and preferred shares combined, he did not own a majority of the common stock. Morgan countered Harriman's majority ownership by having the Northern Pacific's board of directors exercise an option to retire the preferred stock. This action diluted Harriman's holdings to less than a majority.

As the price of Northern Pacific stock rose, the short sellers sensed an opportunity and began to enter the fray; the price did rise, eventually reaching more than $700 a share. All of the shares, however, were owned by the two contending groups, who, at one point, owned by contract even more than the total number of shares outstanding. This presented a problem: From whom would the short sellers borrow shares? Certainly not from the contestants in the takeover battle. As a corner was created, the short sellers were forced to sell other stocks to finance the repurchase of Northern Pacific shares, and a general market panic resulted.

Then on May 9, 1901, a strange turn of events occurred: the Hill and Harriman groups agreed to a truce. A new company, Northern Securities Company, was formed. Each group would have equal representation in the holding company, which would own all of the railroad properties in question. Although the agreement would also permit the short sellers to borrow Northern Pacific shares at $150, the damage to the market had been done. The trading volume on the New York Stock Exchange on that day reached 3,120,000 shares, a record at that time. Again the short sellers were the losers, but in this case the corner resulted in a partial victory. Though neither the Hill-Morgan team nor the Harriman-Schiff team accomplished its original goal, they came out of the action with a profitable, workable agreement. Kuhn Loeb, under Schiff, had established itself as an innovator in the industry and would, with the tacit agreement of J. P. Morgan, be the leading investment banker for the railroad industry for many years. J. P. Morgan & Company would remain the dominant factor in investment banking for industrial corporation and public utilities.

JAY GOULD AND THE GOLD CORNER

The greatest corner in the history of American finance was not attempted on stock but rather on gold, the mysterious precious metal that Shakespeare, in *Romeo and Juliet*, described as "saint seducing." The leading player in this corner, however, was never compared to a saint. The descriptions of Jay Gould ranged from praise for his business acumen ("the smartest man in Wall Street") to far less flattering portrayals of his activities ("a cheat of monstrous proportions"). His personal attributes are not important to this story, but the panic that his actions caused created a major chapter in the financial history of the United States. As with previous similar situations, short sellers played a major role.

In 1869, Jay Gould set out to corner the market in gold. Using several agents to disguise his plan, he amassed contracts to deliver gold valued at nearly $50 million. This was a most interesting figure, since the available supply of gold was estimated to be worth no more than $20 million. Obviously, many who sold him these delivery contracts were selling short. Most of the gold supply at that time was actually held by the U.S. government, which had expressed no intention of selling any of its hoard. Gould was reputed to be very close to government officials, including a relative of the current president, Ulysses S. Grant.

As the price of gold rose, Gould continued to buy and at one point had contracts for delivery of some $100 million worth of the metal. On Thursday, September 23, 1869, Gould sold his entire position at the high of the market, having made many of his sales to one of his unfortunate associates, Jim Fisk. On Friday, September 24, 1869, the U.S. government announced its intention to sell part of its gold store. Panic ensued. The price fell dramatically as brokers began dumping their holdings on the market. By day's end, the value of gold had declined almost $30 an ounce; the day would forever be labeled in history as Black Friday.

Gould profited greatly by selling before the government announcement, but Fisk and many others were ruined. The financial panic that followed destroyed many businesses and left an indelible mark on history—all caused by a frenzy for gold. Perhaps

words written over 350 years earlier by Thomas More in his
Utopia were more prophetic than this great man could ever have
expected.

> They wonder much to hear that gold, which in itself is so useless
> a thing, should be everywhere so much esteemed, that even men
> for whom it was made, and by whom it has its value, should yet
> be thought of less value than it is.

THE CRASH OF 1929

To all students of Wall Street, the crash of 1929 remains the pre-
mier event in the chronicle of twentieth century markets. The crash
did not occur in one day, but instead encompassed a period of six
business days—Wednesday, October 23, through Tuesday, October
29. (The market was open for trading on Saturday during this
period.)

Earlier in the month, the market as measured by the Dow Jones
Industrial Average had experienced a modest and orderly rise and
closed at 352.86 on Thursday, October 10. In the ten days following, a decline occurred but with no noticeable increase in the volume of trading. On Tuesday, October 22, the Dow Jones Industrial
Average closed at 326.51, down 26.35 from the October 10 high.
Total trading volume was 4,130,000 shares. On the following day,
the landslide began in earnest. Volume increased to 6,369,000
shares, and the Dow closed down 20.66 points at 305.85. Thursday, the drop was far more severe. At one point during the day,
the market was down 33.53 to 272.32, before a late rally brought
the market up to 299.47 at the close. The volume reached the unprecedented level of 12,895,000 shares.

The ticker tape that recorded the transactions ran more than an
hour behind so that prices being viewed by traders and investors
had little or no relevance to the current prices of their holdings.
The ticker, which had been introduced to exchange trading in 1867,
had always been able to keep up with the trading activity. (A major contributor to the development of the ticker was Thomas Alva

Edison, then a very young man.) Thursday, October 24, 1929, became forever known as Black Thursday.

Trading on Friday and Saturday were relatively quiet, and after the Sunday holiday, the market approached Monday's opening with the Dow Jones Industrial Average standing at 298.97.

Many of the great names in investment banking had stepped in to stem the decline. Richard Whitney, Thomas W. Lamont, and heads of the major New York City banks attempted to calm the public fears by placing large buy orders in a show of confidence. But a calm was not to be. The public, in panic, was selling whatever holdings it had. Many were forced to sell, as the margin requirements of the day permitted them to buy stocks by putting up as little as 10 percent of the total cost. Their equity had already been wiped out by the decline, leaving them not only losers but often deeply in debt. The short sellers, with no restraints on their activity, fueled the fire, and fortunes and lifelong savings were erased without distinction.

The climax of Monday and Tuesday, October 28 and 29, destroyed whatever hope had remained. Despite the efforts of the money men, the market declined a total of 68.90 over that period, closing at 230.07. In a period of six trading days, the market lost 96.44 points, which represented 30 percent of its value. The volume of trading had soared, reaching 16,410,000 shares on Tuesday, October 29, a figure that would not be surpassed for almost forty years. After an unimpressive rally on Wednesday and Thursday, the Exchange voted to close on Friday and Saturday to allow the firms to sort out their paperwork. But it was too late; the damage had been done. Loans once fully secured by stocks were now in default. Both the borrowers and the lenders suffered great injury, which reflected directly on the nation's economy. While not the only factor, the events on Wall Street during these few days played a large part in the depression that followed. It would require a world war to return prosperity to the United States. This was, indeed, a very costly price to pay.

When measured against later events, the crash of October 1929 may seem minor. On two more recent business days in 1987—Friday, October 16, and Monday, October 19—the market declined over 600 points on the Dow Jones Industrial Average. Current times, however, are not comparable to those of the late 1920s and early 1930s. In 1987, the level from which the decline began was many times higher, and the trading volume averaged about 150 million shares a day. Current credit restrictions are also much more effective, with a minimum of a 50 percent deposit required to purchase stocks. These differences do not minimize the gravity of the 1987 crash. It has justifiably been the subject of many studies and has caused many changes in commercial and investment banking; it was a momentous event that will be indelibly etched in the nation's history. Its causes and effects, however, were different from those of the 1929 market crash. The events of the 1920s led to the arrival of the regulators.

THE SEC IS BORN

In 1933, the Senate Banking and Commerce Committee began an investigation into the activities of securities markets and stock exchanges. The counsel for the committee was Ferdinand Pecora, a highly regarded assistant district attorney for New York City. Testimony was taken from many Wall Street notables, including J. P. Morgan, Jr. It was during this hearing that the famous photograph was taken of Morgan with a midget from the Ringling Brothers Barnum and Bailey Circus seated upon his knee. The disclosures made during these much-publicized hearings would lead to major reforms in the investment community. For the first time, federal laws would regulate the issuing of securities to the public and the conduct of securities markets. Though the major credit for the success of the investigation is deservedly given to Pecora, many other figures were to play important roles in the drafting of the legislation. The leading force was Felix Frankfurter, then a distinguished attorney and professor of law at Harvard and later a Justice of the Supreme Court of the United States.

Two federal securities laws were enacted in a period of just over one year. The Securities Act of 1933, passed on May 27, 1933, primarily addressed the offering of new securities to the public. More than one-half of such securities issued in the 1920s later proved to be worthless, and protection against fraud was obviously needed. This bill, sometimes referred to as the Full Disclosure Law, required an issuer of securities to provide all information about the company to the public. Upon studying this data, investors could determine whether the security was suitable for their purposes. Initially, the Securities Act of 1933 was administered by the Federal Trade Commission (FTC). This function was later transferred to the Securities and Exchange Commission (SEC).

The more-inclusive law, the Securities Exchange Act of 1934, was signed by newly elected President Franklin D. Roosevelt in June 1934. While the major body of securities regulations stems directly or indirectly from this bill, the most important provision was the creation of the Securities and Exchange Commission. The SEC was given virtually unlimited authority to govern the entire securities industry. Initially, the stock exchanges were required to register with the SEC and were then permitted to regulate their members under the direction of the SEC. Under later amendments to the 1934 act, this self-regulatory mechanism was expanded. In 1938, the Maloney Act Amendment authorized the establishment of the National Association of Securities Dealers (NASD), which regulates the over-the-counter (nonexchange) markets. The Securities Act Amendment of 1975 created the Municipal Securities Rulemaking Board (MSRB), which monitors the activity of the municipal bond markets.

The SEC was to consist of five commissioners, and the selection of the first five by President Franklin D. Roosevelt would include one surprise nominee. Three of the commissioners were transferred from the FTC—James Landis, George Matthews, and Robert Healy; the fourth, Ferdinand Pecora, had headed the earlier investigations that led to the birth of the SEC. Roosevelt's fifth nominee was Joseph P. Kennedy, whose son, John F. Kennedy, would be elected as president of the United States in 1960.

The selection of Kennedy surprised most observers and shocked some. Joseph P. Kennedy had left Boston in 1924 to carve out a fortune in Wall Street. His success probably exceeded even his own expectations as he became one of the most prominent stock manipulators in the nation's markets. He is said to have operated on both sides of bear raids, as short seller and defender, and to have participated in numerous pools designed to control stock prices. Kennedy was a loyal Democrat and a major contributor to

Roosevelt's 1932 campaign, but critics still questioned the appointment of a known market opportunist to the lofty position of first chairman of the SEC. Could such a manipulator be effective in curbing his fellow manipulators?

In time, Roosevelt's judgment proved to be more than sound. Although Kennedy's appointment as chairman irritated many constituents, particularly Ferdinand Pecora, Kennedy proved to be a most gifted and devoted public servant. Although he remained in his position for only slightly over one year, Kennedy led the new SEC with an iron hand along a path of structured effectiveness. His prior Wall Street experience was a positive factor. He knew all the games that had been played. He therefore knew what rules were needed to change the outcomes.

Kennedy may have harbored some personal resentment for the Wall Street establishment, which provided additional impetus for his campaign of reform. He had begun his career in Boston in 1922 and made his first major impression in 1924 when he defended the Yellow Cab Company and its owner, John D. Hertz, against a bear raid. Although a later price decline in Yellow Cab stock was reputed to have been engineered by Kennedy, the accusation was never proven. It did, however, demonstrate Mr. Kennedy's adaptability. He could play the game from either side of the court.

In 1926, Kennedy moved his family to a suburb of New York City to be closer to the center of the arena—Wall Street. His reputation continued to grow. In addition to his obvious talents as a trader of securities, Kennedy was endowed with social qualities that enabled him to mingle easily with the raucous traders on the Exchange floor and yet to be equally comfortable with the hierarchy of the investment world. Although his name and fortune were made through market manipulations that might be prohibited today, these manipulations were standard and legal practices in his time. Not even his most consistent opponents ever questioned the integrity of Joseph P. Kennedy.

By 1929, with his reputation firmly established, Kennedy took a bold step. He appeared unannounced at the office of J. P. Morgan & Company and asked to see J. P. Morgan, Jr., himself. Kennedy had perhaps not properly interpreted the social divisions worshiped by the self-described elite to which Morgan belonged.

Kennedy may have been a millionaire, a prominent trader, and a man possessed of a rare financial acumen, but despite his Harvard education he was still an Irish Catholic from Boston. J. P. Morgan declined to see him.

Although much of the credit for the early success of the SEC is deservedly attributed to Joseph Kennedy, one of his most astute accomplishments was the staff he built to support his efforts. One staff member, William O. Douglas, was a young law professor from New England when he was appointed to study the bankruptcy and reorganization section of the 1934 act. Douglas would eventually be appointed the third chairman of the SEC and would later distinguish himself as a justice of the Supreme Court of the United States.

REFORMING THE EXCHANGES

One of the main goals of the new SEC was the reform of the stock exchanges. At this time there were twenty-four exchanges located in various cities throughout the country. The New York Mining Exchange and the Boston Curb Exchange would be forced to close, while the others would be required to register with the SEC.

The greatest challenge was to force a reorganization of the New York Stock Exchange, the location of most of the abusive manipulation of the past. But the Exchange was rich and powerful and fought off all attempts to institute meaningful reforms. For years the president of the Exchange, Richard Whitney, was able to thwart every move by the SEC. It was not until November 1937, under the chairmanship of Douglas, that the SEC's efforts began to bear fruit. Douglas in effect offered the Exchange two choices: reform or be taken over by the government. An Exchange committee was formed to revise its organization, and it presented a plan that would establish an entirely new board of governors, which would include public representatives. The plan was approved, and the new board was sworn in in May 1938. Its first president was William McChesney Martin, Jr., who had been the architect of the reform program.

Two months earlier however, on March 8, 1938, a remarkable event had occurred. The Exchange had suspended Richard Whitney and Company for conduct inconsistent with just and equitable principles of trade. A few days later, Richard Whitney himself was expelled from Exchange membership for similar violations.

Whitney had been accused of misappropriating funds from customers' accounts and monies from the Exchanges Gratuity Fund, of which he was the custodian. The mighty had fallen. Richard Whitney, bond broker for J. P. Morgan and president of the NYSE during the crash of 1929 and its years of turmoil, had been destroyed and had become an outcast and a bankrupt. Whitney served three years in prison before achieving parole in 1941. Although he lived for thirty-three years after his discharge, he was never involved in financial matters again.

The early years of the SEC saw the enactment of many laws and industry regulations that changed the face of financial markets. Under the first three chairmen—Kennedy, Landis, and Douglas—much was accomplished. But as old abuses were controlled, new ones were born, and the challenge to the regulators continues today. Ferdinand Pecora, who provided the initial force that resulted in reform, served for only six months as a commissioner. He then embarked on a noted career in the judiciary. Kennedy reigned for fourteen months, but his accomplishments were just beginning. He later became the U.S. ambassador to the Court of Saint James's and continued to enhance his reputation as a businessman. His family would fill many pages of the history of the United States. Their triumphs and tragedies are covered in many other volumes. In fact, as important as Joseph P. Kennedy was to the history of Wall Street, his chairmanship of the SEC was merely a brief, though noteworthy, incident in his life.

4

The Laws, the Rules, the Results

Although the work of the SEC began with the enactment of the Securities Exchange Act of 1934 (properly titled the Rayburn–Fletcher Act after its congressional sponsors), it was not until 1938 that a rule was enacted to prevent bear raids.

For a bear raider to be successful, he must force down the price of the stock through short sales. Once the trend is set in motion, he can cease selling and allow public sellers to accelerate the decline. As the price drops further, the bear raider repurchases the stock (covers the short) at profitable bargain prices. At times, raiders gained control of a company at levels well below true value. The basic theory of a bear raid, however, is that the stock must be placed under selling pressure: At first, short sales are made at successively lower prices. Later, the short seller buys at the lower prices created by the original short sales.

SEC Rules 10a-1 and 10a-2, enacted in 1938 and amended in 1939, made such activities illegal. These rules limited short sales to situations in which the price of the stock was rising—quite the opposite of the bear raiders' intentions. Under these rules, a short seller could never initiate a price decline. The rules applied only to transactions on stock exchanges, since over-the-counter (nonexchange) trades could not be adequately monitored at this point in history.

THE PLUS TICK RULE

In effect, SEC Rules 10a-1 and 10a-2 and later exchange regulations stated the following: "All short sales on stock exchanges must be made at a price higher than the last sale or last different sale."

The rule is commonly referred to as the *plus tick* rule. The term *plus tick* may require a bit of explanation. In 1867 the stock ticker was introduced on the New York Stock Exchange. This remarkable device allowed each transaction on the Exchange to be recorded in sequence. The prices were typed on a keyboard and then reproduced on a long, thin strip of paper, which flowed from a small printing device. Because the machine made a clicking sound as it fed out the prices, each transaction in a stock was called a "tick." So, plus tick simply means a plus transaction.

When an order to sell stock short on the Exchange floor is entered, it must be clearly marked as a short sale. This informs the broker on the floor that execution of the order requires a plus tick.

THE SHORT SELLING TRANSACTION

Suppose that a customer, John J. Client, wishes to sell short 100 shares of XYZ stock at the market. Mr. Client wishes to profit from an anticipated decline in the stock. He will sell the stock today and repurchase it later at a lower price. He gives the order to his brokerage firm, which then prepares the order and transmits it to the Exchange floor (see Figure 4.1).

Once transmitted to the Exchange floor, the order is given to a broker—let's call him Broker A—who handles the execution. On the Exchange floor, all stocks are traded at a particular location known as a *trading post*. Broker A goes to the post location where XYZ stock is traded; there he finds another broker, also an Exchange member, who is called a *specialist*. The specialist is responsible for maintaining an orderly market in a security. A specialist's function is not to prevent a stock price from rising or falling, but rather to attempt to see that market fluctuations are orderly. While this is not always possible, it is nonetheless the floor specialist's job.

Broker A wants a quotation on XYZ stock and addresses the specialist as follows:

How's XYZ?

The specialist replies as follows:

68 - 68 1/2
5 By 10

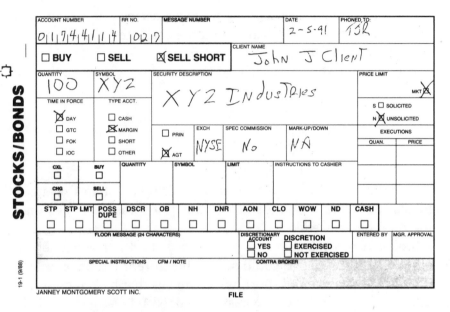

Figure 4.1. Short sale of 100 shares of XYZ Company stock at the market. (Copyright Janney Montgomery Scott Inc. Reproduced by permission.)
Note: On the upper center, the order is marked "SHORT." The location of the transaction, "NYSE," is indicated in the box labeled "EXCH." In the middle left, the order is designated as "DAY," which means that if it is not executed on this business day it will automatically expire. Had the box marked "GTC" been checked, the order would have been "good til canceled" by the customer or executed. The order ticket further indicates the number of shares, the symbol for the stock, and the price:

100   XYZ   Mkt

A market order instructs the broker to obtain the best available price with no specific limitations.

Other information on the order indicates the customer's name and account number and the fact that the order is being entered for the customer's margin account. A later discussion of margin regulations regarding securities will explain that all short sales must be made in a margin account.

The specialist has told Broker A that the highest price anyone is willing to pay for XYZ stock (the bid) is $68 a share. The lowest price at which anyone will sell at this time (the offer) is $68.50 a share. The phrase "5 By 10" indicates that the price of $68 will be paid for up to 500 shares and that 1,000 shares are offered for sale at $68.50.

Above each trading post a monitor indicates the price of the most recent transaction in each stock and the character of that transaction, plus or minus.

The monitor shows the following:

XYZ

−

68 1/4

This indicates that the past price at which XYZ shares changed hands was $68.25 a share and that this price was lower (−) than the one that preceded it.

Broker A has 100 shares of XYZ to sell short at the market. In other circumstances he could sell at the current bid price of $68. But his order is marked short, which means that he is required to sell on a plus tick. Since the past price of 68 1/4 was a minus tick, he must offer his stock at a higher price. Remember the plus tick rule: a short sale must be made at a price higher than the last different price.

He offers the 100 shares at 68 3/8 as follows:

100 XYZ at 68 3/8

Broker B, who has an order to buy 100 shares of XYZ at market, accepts this offer; a transaction takes place at 68 3/8. Since this was a higher price than the previous sale of 68 1/4, it is called a plus tick (+). The last sale monitor would now read:

XYZ
+
68 3/8

The sale by Broker A complied with the short sale rule since it was made at a price higher than the previous sale.

Suppose Broker C now arrives at the trading post. He also has an order to sell:

100   XYZ   Market   Short

He consults the monitor and notes that the last sale, 68 3/8, was a plus tick. He knows that under the rules he can sell short at the same price. Broker C therefore offers his stock as follows:

100 XYZ at 68 3/8

Broker D accepts his offer, and another transaction takes place at 68 3/8. This transaction is known as a *zero-plus tick* (0+). The price is unchanged from the last transaction, but higher than the price of the last *different* transaction. Our sequence of prices appears as follows:

–	+	0+
68 1/4	68 3/8	68 3/8

Both transactions at 68 3/8 are legitimate short sales since they were made at a price higher than the last sale or last different sale. In the example, a short seller could offer stock at 68 3/8 continuously since each transaction would qualify as a zero-plus tick.

By law, no action by a short seller can cause a decline in the price of the stock. Hence, bear raids, as they were conducted in earlier years, are now illegal. Short sellers can still profit from price declines, but they cannot create them.

To test your knowledge of this rule, look at this sequence of transactions in MNO stock. Which of them could have been short sales?

–	0–	+	+	0+	–
38	38	38 1/8	38 1/4	38 1/4	38

Only the 38 1/8 and the two 38 1/4 trades could have been short sales, as they were at plus or zero-plus prices. In each case stock was sold at rising prices. This is not what the bear raider desires.

Note that the short seller is never required to disclose the fact that he is selling short. In fact, the buyer does not even care. The buyer's concern is that the shares are delivered to him according to the terms of the contract. The short seller will accomplish this by borrowing the stock from someone who owns it. This process will be explained in more detail in a later chapter.

When stock is sold, the seller is said to be either long or short. A long seller owns the shares and will deliver them to the buyer. A short seller does not intend to deliver his own stock, but will deliver borrowed shares. A long seller can sell at any price; a short seller can sell only on a plus tick or a zero plus tick.

RUMOR SPREADING AND INSIDER TRADING

While the plus tick rule may have closed one avenue used to artificially depress the price of a stock, the investor must be on guard against other illegal and perhaps more difficult-to-detect practices. A person or group seeking a decline in a stock's value might spread false information indicating problems within a corporation. Just as "hot tips," whether true or false, can lead to a sudden surge of buying in a stock, rumors that predict trouble can cause a wave of selling and result in a decline in value. Because many people will happily repeat gossip, no matter how unfounded, information regarding future events within a corporation will spread as if borne by the wind. Fortunately, investors can rely on many reliable research services, who publish information that is thoroughly checked and prepared by professionals. Beware of the confidential information a well-meaning friend may pass on to you. The originator of the story may have had a motive quite different from the one you think.

The 1934 Securities Exchange Act and the SEC also addressed and worked to correct another source of market abuses. Obviously, some people will have access to more of a company's information than is available to the investing public in general. Because these persons can utilize this information for their own financial gain, causing an offsetting loss to others, the SEC sought to identify and regulate these individuals by enacting what has come to be known as the insider rules. While not all of these regulations refer directly to short selling, they are important considerations for anyone contemplating this strategy.

The law defines an *insider* as an officer, director, or holder of 10 percent or more of a corporation's stock. These people are in a position to know details of a corporation's progress well before those details are made available to the public. Clearly, their activities in buying or selling shares of their corporation's stock could be indicative of their knowledge of future events. Therefore, certain regulations have been imposed on insiders:

1. *Insiders must report their holdings in the company's stock to the SEC.* If you are elected to the board of directors of General Motors next week, you must report to the SEC the number of shares of that company's stock that you own either directly or beneficially. The size of your position might permit investors to interpret your degree of personal commitment to the corporation.

2. *Insiders must report any change in their holdings to the SEC.* Once a person has registered as an insider, he must continually report increases or decreases in his holdings. Within any month that an insider buys or sell shares, a report giving the details of these transactions must be made by the tenth day of the following month. These reports are made public and are carried by the financial press. If large purchases are reported by a number of company insiders, the purchases may indicate the insiders' feelings of forthcoming prosperity for that corporation. This could be a factor in an investor's decision to purchase shares. On the other hand, if the report shows a rash of selling by insiders, the investor should be cautious. If the people directly involved in corporate affairs are "bailing out," it may not be wise to purchase this stock. In another case, a reader of the report may already own shares of the company. If the insiders are selling, perhaps she should follow their lead. A speculator might view this insider selling as an indication that a short sale is in order. Perhaps the corporate sellers are aware of bad news in the future. Perhaps a short sale made now can be covered later at a lower price, thereby yielding a generous profit.

Take caution in interpreting these reports, however; their underlying meanings may not be as obvious as they seem. Insiders might sell for reasons other than a bleak corporate outlook. Often the holding of a corporation's stock is an insider's principal asset. He may have financial needs that can only be met by liquidating some of his position. The chairman of the board, for example, may be a multimillionaire based on the value of the stock he owns, but his wealth is only on paper. While the stock may provide some income through dividend payments, it may not provide for all of his needs. He may need cash for a new home, college costs for children, or other expenses. He may simply wish to diversify his holdings. Having all one's eggs in one basket is usually not a wise approach to investing. Perhaps the chairman wants to add some municipal securities to his portfolio to earn tax-exempt income. So while it is important to be aware of insider trades, such trades are not the only basis from which to draw conclusions.

The entire insider trading report is available each month from the SEC. Most brokerage firms have copies on hand, and investors would be wise to check the activity in stock that they own or contemplate purchasing. Short sellers should certainly consult this information before taking or continuing a short position.

While the financial sections do not publish the entire insider report, they do provide a revealing concentration of the important data. Figure 4.2 is an example.

3. *Insiders cannot take short-term profits on the sale of their company's stock.* The board of directors of XYZ Corporation is holding a meeting this morning. All directors are smiling as they learn the results of the recently ended quarter. The earnings are double those of the prior quarter, and orders for future delivery are running at a record pace. The earnings will probably double again in the next quarter. The board of directors decides to share this success with the stockholders by voting to substantially increase the dividend. They call a press conference to announce the increase at 4:00 P.M. that afternoon. At this point, only the men

INSIDER TRADING SPOTLIGHT

Biggest Individual Trades

(Based on reports filed with regulators last week)

COMPANY NAME	EXCH.	INSIDER'S NAME[1]	TITLE[2]	$ VALUE (000)	NO. OF SHRS. IN TRANS. (000)	% OF HLDNG.	TRANSACTION DATES
BUYERS							
Natl Commerce Bancorp	O	T.M. Garrott x	P	1,627	78.3	34	5/21-29/90
BMR Financial	O	J.L. Greene	O	1,137	135.0	50	4/10-19/90
Agnico-Eagle Mines	O	M. Drutz	D	745	84.0	27	5/22/90
Comstock Resources	O	H.C. Pell III x	D	659	109.8	136	4/11/90
Natl Education	N	R.C. Blum x	D	615	140.5	11	5/4-8/90
Valhi	N	H.C. Simmons x	D	568	38.0	Q	5/1-23/90
Michigan Natl	O	E.D. Prince	D	529	15.0	14	5/15/90
Caere	O	S.S. Kahn	D	500	20.0	Q	4/11/90
Bio-Tech Genl	O	D. Tolkowsky x	D	458	200.0	489	5/4-22/90
Laserscope	O	R.G. Jagunich	VP	420	20.0	48	5/18/90
SELLERS							
Fruit of the Loom	A	W.F. Farley s	CB	8,137	594.8	43	5/8-31/90
Blockbuster Ent	N	J.J. Shearer	VP	6,241	275.0	44	5/18-31/90
McCaw Cellular Comm	O	W.M. Perry s	D	5,561	200.0	99	5/21-31/90
Apple Computer	O	J. Sculley	CB	4,932	120.0	31	5/7-8/90
Humana	N	D.A. Jones s	CB	4,563	100.0	4	5/21/90
Acuson	N	K.H. Johannsmeier	D	4,111	100.0	3	5/22-24/90
Waste Mgmt	N	P.B. Rooney	P	3,303	89.0	11	5/8-9/90
Limited	N	T.B. Lyons	O	3,280	69.0	100	5/23/90
Natl Media	O	A.J. Salaman	D	2,937	320.0	24	5/4-9/90
Aldus	O	P. Brainerd	P	2,681	100.0	3	5/22-23/90

Companies With Biggest Net Changes

(Based on actual transaction dates in reports filed through last Friday)

COMPANY NAME	EXCH.	NET % CHG. IN HOLDINGS OF ACTIVE INSIDERS[3] LATEST 8 WEEKS	NET % CHG. IN HOLDINGS OF ACTIVE INSIDERS[3] LATEST 24 WEEKS	LATEST 8 WKS. NO. OF BUYERS- SELLERS	LATEST 8 WKS. MULTIPLE OF HIST. NORM[4]	LATEST 24 WKS. NO. OF BUYERS- SELLERS	LATEST 24 WKS. MULTIPLE OF HIST. NORM[4]
BUYING							
Holnam	N	49900	1315	4-0	1.0	5-0	1.0
Aerovox	O	400	400	8-0	1.0	8-0	1.0
AMR (Del)	N	113	148	2-0	9.0	4-0	6.0
Pacific Ent	N	107	276	3-0	4.2	4-0	1.8
Southeast Banking	N	86	85	3-0	3.9	6-0	2.6
Louisville Gas & Elec	N	85	158	3-0	27.0	5-1	15.0
CoreStates Financial	O	84	30	7-0	2.0	9-0	0.9
Conservative Savings	O	77	84	4-0	1.0	5-0	1.0
Vorthen Banking	A	65	72	2-0	3.6	5-0	3.0
Alatenn Resources	O	57	67	5-0	18.0	5-0	6.0
SELLING							
Healthdyne	O	− 96	− 62	0-2	3.3	0-3	1.6
Policy Mgmt Systems	O	− 86	− 74	0-2	1.5	0-4	1.0
Baker Hughes	N	− 84	− 84	0-5	8.8*	1-5	2.9
Quantum	O	− 75	− 81	0-4	4.2	0-8	2.8
Pyramid Tech	O	− 64	− 64	0-4	4.8	1-4	1.6
Kimberly-Clark	N	− 63	− 57	0-2	4.0	2-2	1.3
Lukens	N	− 56	− 25	0-2	2.6	1-3	1.3
AT&E	A	− 51	− 22	0-3	9.0	1-3	3.0
Chemfix Tech	O	− 49	− 38	0-2	2.3	0-3	1.1
Caterpillar	N	− 40	− 41	0-2	1.2	0-4	0.8

NOTE: Shows purchases and sales by officers and directors, which must be reported to the SEC, FDIC, FHLBB by the 10th of the month following the month of the trade. Includes open-market and private transactions involving direct and indirect holdings. Excludes stocks valued at less than $2 a share, acquisitions through options or stock splits, gifts, and companies being acquired. Individuals are ranked by the dollar value of their transactions. Q=No prior holdings.
[1]x=Reflects, or includes, shares held indirectly. s=Also holds other class of stock.
[2]CB=chairman. P=president. D=director. VP=vice president. O=officer. Z=other.
[3]Ranked by the net change in shares held by all insiders who bought or sold during the latest eight weeks, expressed as a percentage of their total holdings at the start of the period. Reflects companies for which filings made last week showed some insider activity during the latest eight weeks. Excluded: companies with total purchases valued under $50,000 or total sales valued under $100,000; companies with only one buyer or seller, or fewer buyers or sellers than the historical average for the period.
[4]The number of buyers or sellers as a multiple of the historical average for the period, based on the previous three calendar years.   *Base period is less than three years.   Source: Invest/Net, North Miami, Fla.

Figure 4.2. Typical listing of major insider trades from the financial page of a daily newspaper. (Copyright 1990, the Wall Street Journal. Reproduced by permission.)

and women in this conference room are aware of this spectacular corporate news.

One of the listeners is Director Jones. He has been promising his family a vacation to Australia and New Zealand for months, but the expense of such a venture frightens him. Now he sees a way to pay painlessly for the excursion. When this news is announced, the price of XYZ stock will certainly react. In Jones's opinion, it should rise 4 or perhaps 5 points a share. As soon as the board meeting ends, he runs to his office, calls his broker, and buys 5,000 shares of XYZ Corporation stock. As he predicted, the share price rises on the good news, and a few days later he sells the stock for a profit of $25,000. Off to the Pacific flies the Jones family. Director Jones is a happy man.

Director Jones's happiness, however, does not last for long. The rules governing insiders, such as Director Jones, prohibit them from taking profits in their company's stock within a period of six months from the date of purchase. Once his profit is detected, which can be done from the published insider reports, Director Jones is subject for suit to return the profit to the treasury of the XYZ Corporation.

This regulation may impose some limitations on normal trading practices for insiders, but it certainly protects the public investor from damage. Jones may have purchased his 5,000 shares from investor Smith, who certainly would not have sold them had she had the same information that the director possessed.

4. *Insiders cannot sell their company's stock short.* Suppose the news at that XYZ board meeting is all bad. Not only will earnings for the quarter be down, but there will be no earnings at all. The corporation will report a huge loss for the period. With this in mind, the directors vote to eliminate the dividend. The stockholders will be very unhappy, many will sell their shares and the price will surely decline. But it will be many hours before this news is made public. Director Jones still sees a direct route to Australia. He calls his broker and places an order to short sell 5,000 shares of XYZ Corporation. When the price declines in response to the news, he covers the short at a large profit and begins to pack his bags. The investor who purchased the stock from him has a loss that equals Jones's profit. In reality, however, this will not happen. The insider rules prohibit the short sale of stock by these parties. They are not permitted to use non-public informatin—good or bad—to their advantage and to the detriment of the public.

"Insiders" on the Outside

In addition to corporate insiders, other people—underwriters of securities, accounts, stockbrokers—may also be privy to exclusive information. Therefore, the definition of an insider was expanded to include "anyone who is privy to nonpublic information." Such people are not permitted to make improper use of this informa-tion subject to the penalties of the laws. These penalties were sharply increased under the Insider Trading Law of 1988. This law calls for a maximum of ten years in prison and a $1 million fine for violations by individuals. The fine increases to $2.5 million if the violator is a partnership or corporation.

In recent years, charges of insider trading have been leveled against a variety of people. For example, an employee of a print-ing company was accused of improperly using information that came before him in the course of his work. The violation concerned what is referred to as a *tender offer*. If a person or a corporation wishes to acquire a large position in a company's stock, that per-son or corporation can invite shareholders to sell, or tender, their stock. To make the deal attractive, the buyer offers a much higher price than the current market value. If the stock is now trading at $45 a share, the party making the tender offer might agree to pay $55 a share. Why is the buyer willing to pay so high a price? Per-haps his goal is to purchase 20 percent of the outstanding stock. This may not be possible in the open market, or may require that he pay even higher prices. The tender offer may prove to be a more economical approach. Naturally, when the offer is announced the price of the stock will rise.

Since these offers are announced through advertisements in the financial press, they are first routed through the buyer's agent to be prepared for publication. The printer mentioned earlier saw the terms of a deal before it was publicly announced. He purchased stock for himself and others and sold at a profit when the news came out. The information on which he acted was not public at the time. He therefore made improper use of this information, and was charged with insider trading.

Tender offers are also subject to SEC Rule 10b-4 which governs short sellers. When a tender offer is made, the price of the stock rises. In the previous example, when the tender offer was made at $55 a share, the price was expected to go up. It might not have increased as high as $55, because our buyer in this instance wanted only 20 percent of the stock. History tells us, however, that once the tender offer is completed, the price usually declines. This would seem to provide a golden opportunity for a short seller. He arranges to borrow 1,000 shares of the stock in question and tenders it at $55 a share. Perhaps not all of the shares will be accepted, but suppose 500 shares are taken at the tender price. He returns the other 500 shares to the lender and then waits. When the tender offer ends, the stock price declines to, perhaps, $47 a share in the open market. He buys 500 shares at that price, returns it to the lender, and shows a gross profit of $8 a share, or $4,000, for his efforts. This sounds like an easy way for a short seller to make money, but SEC Rule 10b-4 prohibits this practice.

Briefly, the rule requires that any person who responds to a tender offer must be a long seller, or own the shares. A person cannot tender borrowed stock. This would deprive the true owners of the stock of the opportunity to have their shares accepted.

Suffice it to say that just about anyone could be considered an insider. To use an extreme example, a maintenance worker is repairing a broken electrical outlet in the office of an attorney, who is working on the details of a yet-to-be-announced merger between two corporations. The news, when announced, will lead to a rise in the price of one or both of the companies involved. The attorney has carelessly left the documents detailing the terms of the deal on his desk. A curious electrician reads the material, grasps the ramifications, and buys some stock. With the profits, he buys his own building and hires someone else to do the electrical work.

Being an insider is not a violation of any rule. It only means that you are privy to nonpublic information. It is the improper use of this information that constitutes a crime.

Short sellers are often the victims of insider trading. A rapid rise in the price of a stock often attracts short sales. Analysis of the company in question may lead a trader to the conclusion that the price has gone too high, and a short sale might be in order. But if the increase was caused by insider buying based on nonpublic information, that short seller might be falling into a trap. By the time he learns the facts, it is too late. The price has gone still higher, and he has a large loss. The game, however, was not played fairly. The short seller played by the rules; the insider did not.

If a person must report as an insider when she attains a position of 10 percent or more of a company's stock, what of the person who owns 9 percent, 8 percent, or 7 percent? By definition, that person is not an insider, but her position is quite significant. All investors, short sellers included, would find such information important, but no report must be made under the insider requirements.

Still another regulation (SEC Rule 13D) covers such situations. Under this rule, a report must be filed by any party who owns 5 percent or more of a company's stock. In addition, the party must disclose his intentions:

Does he plan to hold the 5 percent as an investment?

Does he plan to increase his holdings to 20 percent?

Does he plan to attempt to purchase 100 percent of the stock?

Certainly this information is of great importance to investors. If a major corporation has disclosed a plan to make large purchases of some other corporation's stock, some people might be disposed to purchase the stock themselves. By the same token, a short sale of the shares being accumulated might be a very unwise move.

Market analysts and investors alike study these Rule 13D filings intently. Some manipulators, however, would like to acquire large positions but avoid the reporting requirements.

STOCK PARKING

During the stock market scandals of the 1980s, one of the illegal practices discovered was called *stock parking*. Investor A wishes to acquire a large interest in XYZ Corporation. He believes that if he can accumulate 20 percent of the company's shares, he can control the entire corporation and then threaten the management unless his stock is purchased from him at a substantially higher price. If he is required to report when his position reaches 5 percent, however, his intentions will be known to all. This will attract other buyers, and Investor A might be unable to attain his goal. So he sets about "parking" the stock. He enlists the services of investors B, C, D, and E. As he accumulates shares, he sells them privately to his coconspirators. He pays his cohorts for their efforts and indemnifies them against any loss. In time, each investor—A, B, C, D, and E—is registered as an owner of 4 percent of the stock of the XYZ Corporation. No report is required since the 5 percent level has not been reached. Investor A actually controls 20 percent of the stock, but no one, not potential buyers or sellers, is aware of this fact. This is a fraudulent avoidance of the rules.

During the stock market scandals of the 1980s, the name most prominently mentioned was that of Ivan Boeksy. A market manipulator of epic proportions, Boesky became identified with all of the evils that undermined the confidence of investors. On November 14, 1986, Ivan Boesky pleaded guilty to a number of charges, including insider trading violations and stock parking. Boesky, although he agreed to cooperate with the government in future investigations, was sentenced to federal prison and fined a then record amount of $100 million.

Although a staggering figure, in less than four years later it was made to look almost insignificant. On April 24, 1990, Michael Milken appeared in federal court in New York City and pleaded guilty to a number of violations of securities laws. Among the charges were mail fraud, securities fraud, and conspiracy. Other charges, including insider trading, had not been pressed by the government. The total fines and restitution levied against Milken were $600 million. Was this a monumental amount? By most standards it certainly was, but in Milken's case perhaps the penalty was not that severe. Between 1983 and 1987, Milken was paid $1.1 billion by his employer, the Wall Street firm Drexel Burnham Lambert Inc. This $1.1 billion is exclusive of income Milken earned from other sources.

Michael Milken created a form of financing that used a device called *junk bonds*—low-quality debt securities that pay a higher-than-usual rate of interest. Junk bonds were used to finance corporate takeovers and projects of questionable merit. The implementation of this financing method led to the abuses to which Milken pleaded guilty in 1990. This is not to say that junk bond financing is improper; many worthwhile projects were able to raise needed capital by using this product. The abuses that resulted, however, led to deterioration of markets and a loss of confidence by investors that may never be fully restored.

The real suffering caused by market abuses often escapes notice. The firm of Drexel Burnham Lambert declared bankruptcy early in 1990. A long history of achievement ended abruptly because a small group chose to ignore the rules and ethics of the securities industry. The thousands of people who were left without jobs are seldom mentioned. They were the real victims, and not even $600 million could repair the damage.

So there are rules, insider requirements, filing requirements, and prohibitions against fraud and unfair practices, but there are still people who find ways to avoid these regulations. All investors must exercise extreme care, but the short seller must be even more careful, for he exposes himself to a potentially unlimited loss. The buyer of securities has a risk, but it is measurable; the short seller has a far greater risk. If a person purchases a stock, it can decline only to a value of zero. A short seller, however, must eventually repurchase the shares he has sold at an unknown price. How much can a short seller lose? How high is up?

5

Applications of Selling Short

Thus far most of the discussion has depicted the misuse of short selling—bear raids, insider trading, takeover strategies, and other illegal tactics. This chapter examines selling short as a useful device for market participation. While there are many applications of the short sale, the one most often used is speculation.

SPECULATING BY SELLING SHORT

The concept is simple: if you think that a stock is going up and wish to speculate, purchase the shares; if you believe that the price of a stock is declining, speculate by selling short.

Suppose that early in May, you read the following headline in the financial section of the newspaper: "Big Three Auto Makers Profits Decline Sharply in First Quarter." The accompanying article gives details of lower sales and earnings for General Motors, Ford, and Chrysler. In studying the material, you note that General Motors per-share earnings dropped from $2.37 to $1.02 a share, a decline of more than 54 percent.

You feel that this omen is poor for future sales and conclude that the decline will continue through the next year. This should lead to a decline in the price of these companies' stocks. As a trader, you decide to enter the following short sale order:

Sell   1000   GM   Market   Short

The order reaches the floor of the New York Stock Exchange, and your broker sells the 1,000 shares short on an up-tick at $45 a share. Because you do not own the shares, the brokerage firm arranges to borrow the shares for you. In fact, the firm ascertained its ability to borrow the shares before it entered your order. Borrowing shares of General Motors or other highly capitalized companies usually presents no problem. But in many cases—particularly with over-the-counter securities—shares cannot be borrowed and, thus, short sales cannot be completed.

Now that you have established your position, your account shows you are short 1,000 shares of General Motors stock. You must wait for your prediction of a price decline to fulfill itself. Suppose that it does. A few months later, with car sales continuing to decline, General Motors stock has fallen to $40 a share. Not being greedy, you enter the following order through your broker:

Buy   1000   GM   Market   (CVR SHT)

Your broker buys the shares on the Exchange at $40 a share. You have covered your short. On settlement date, your account is debited for the shares you purchased (approximately $40,000), and you return the shares to the party from whom you borrowed them. Your short sale brought in about $45,000; thus, you had a profit of $5,000 (less commission and other expenses) on the short position. A very nice move on your part. All you did was reverse the usual order of things. You sold first and purchased later. It was just as much of a profit as if you had purchased first and sold later at a price higher than your purchase price.

But different circumstances could lead to an unsatisfactory conclusion. For example, shortly after making your short sale, General Motors introduces a new automobile. It is an instant success, and dealers are taking orders faster than the new vehicles can be manufactured. Sales soar; General Motors earnings rise rapidly;

the future has never looked brighter. Everyone is happy—except for the person who sold General Motors stock short.

The sales and earnings improvement has a positive effect on the price of the stock, which rises to $50 a share. Since you sold 1,000 shares short at $45, you now have a $5,000 loss. What do you do? You decide to wait a little longer. This turns out to be a mistake, because General Motors shares continue to increase to $55. Your loss on paper is now $10,000. You could cover it now and take your loss or continue to hold your position. Perhaps the price will decline and you will be a winner; perhaps not. If General Motors rises to $60, $70, or $80, and you are still short at $45 a share, you may have an ever-increasing loss.

Other events can also have a detrimental effect on investors. Suppose the U.S. government places strict import restrictions on foreign automobiles. The result could be a sharp increase in domestic auto sales. This is good news for American automobile manufacturers, but very bad news for those who sold their shares short.

Changes in the value of the dollar can cause an increase in sales of domestic products; these changes may be positive or negative. The short seller may properly gauge the prospects for a company, based on accepted analytical standards. Outside influences are more difficult to judge, but are equally important.

The decline in tensions between Eastern and Western bloc nations could lead to a sharp reduction in defense spending. This could then cause an erosion of the earnings of major suppliers. Would short sales of these company's shares be appropriate? Perhaps yes, perhaps no. Many of these companies are versatile enough to replace lost defense business with work from the private sector that will result in the development of new consumer products. Their financial picture could improve and, with it, the price of the shares.

There is a risk in every area of investing. Even the buyer of U.S. Treasury securities assumes some risk. Changing interest rates can affect the value of these conservative positions, either positively or negatively.

The short seller is the only market participant who voluntarily assumes unlimited risk. Suppose a client purchases General Motors stock at $45 a share and the stock declines to $40. She shows a loss of $5 a share, but she owns the stock. Every three months, she receives a dividend check, which provides some income. If she needs to borrow money to buy furniture, the stock is usable as collateral for a loan. In time, the shares might rise again in value, and she will have a profit. But her loss potential is limited to the amount she paid to buy the stock.

This is not the case for the short seller; his potential for loss is unlimited. As the stock rises in value, he is called by his broker to deposit additional funds into his account. He can eventually run out of funds and be forced to cover the short at a most inappropriate time. In addition, while the client who bought the stock receives a check every three months, our short seller must pay out the quarterly dividend to the party from whom he borrowed the shares.

Short selling as a speculation can be a profitable market device, but it presents dangers far too great for most investors. As a speculation, the theory is just the reverse of buying shares. If you are bullish, buy. If you are bearish and can shoulder the risk, sell short.

OTHER USES OF SHORT SELLING

Not all short selling is done as a speculation on a market decline. It is often used by professionals as a means of facilitating other transactions. The following are a few examples of this technique.

A major Wall Street firm, Jones & Co., receives a very large order from an institutional client. The client may be a bank or a mutual fund which often deals in huge amounts of stock. The client wishes to purchase 500,000 shares of XYZ common stock at $65 a share. The execution of this order will result in a large commission for Jones & Co., so the firm goes to great lengths to find the stock for the client. Despite all efforts, however, Jones & Co. finds that only 450,000 shares are available at the $65 limit. Should the firm tell the client that it has failed and then surrender the order? Not on your life. It provides the missing 50,000 shares itself by selling the stock short. As a result, Jones & Co. receives the commission on the 500,000 shares from the buyer and perhaps even earns additional commissions by representing some of those who sold the 450,000 shares. The firm has taken on the risk of selling short 50,000 shares and may take a loss on the short position. Jones & Co. hopes, however, that any loss will be more than offset by the commissions earned and that it will still show a profit. There are ways to protect short positions and minimize any possible loss. These will be discussed in a later chapter.

Another professional who often uses short selling to facilitate transactions is the specialist on the New York Stock Exchange, whose job is to maintain an orderly market in a security. If the specialist in IBM stock does his work effectively, the price of IBM shares will rise or fall in an orderly manner. If the price is 109, it may rise on the next transactions to 109 1/4, or it may fall to 108 3/4. However, a sequence of prices such as this would not be seen:

IBM	IBM	IBM	IBM
109	112	106	102

This sequence is not very orderly. Whenever there is a great rush of buying or selling in a stock, the price variations may be greater than normal. But those variations would represent unusual situations. In most markets prices vary continually; but no matter how rapid the changes, they will be gradual.

The specialist plays two roles in the performance of his functions: as agent for others and as principal when buying and selling for his own account. The term *specialist* is used in both the singular sense and the plural sense: he is an individual who stands at the trading post and does the work, but he is also part of a specialist firm that includes many people and controls large amounts of capital. Major firms such as Merrill Lynch, Paine Webber, and Bear Stearns have divisions that act as specialists in listed securities.

When acting as agent, or broker, the specialist handles orders entrusted to him by other firms. For example, Morgan Stanley & Company may have a limit order to sell 1000 shares of IBM at $110. If IBM stock is currently at $109 a share, it would be unwise for Morgan Stanley to position one of its brokers at the trading post to wait for the price to rise. The broker's time could be spent elsewhere more usefully. Generally, the Morgan Stanley broker will give the order to the specialist to handle for the firm. The specialist has what is called the book. He enters into that book Morgan

Stanley's order to sell 1,000 shares of IBM at $110 a share. Other firms will also give him orders to buy or sell at prices below and above the current price. He will act as agent for these firms, and if they wish to sell he will make purchases for those who give him buy orders. The price may decline, but by using these orders the decline will be orderly. On the other hand, if a large number of brokers arrive at the specialist's post wishing to purchase IBM, he can, in part, supply the stock from the sell orders that Morgan Stanley and others have placed on his book. The specialist is merely acting as agent for these firms. He receives a fee called floor brokerage for his work, but his most important contribution is the part he plays in stabilizing market fluctuations.

As in all aspects of the securities industry, the specialists employ a great deal of advanced automation, but the old-fashioned book still exists. Its use is generally restricted, however, to shares that are not actively traded.

Each page of the book represents 1 point for the stock. Figure 5-1 shows the book created for orders in XYZ stock at prices from $81 to $81 7/8 a share.

A study of the book shows that the highest price to buy on the book is 81 1/4. The specialist has orders from four different firms to purchase a total of 1,600 shares at that price. The lowest price at which XYZ is offered for sale is 81 5/8 a share. A total of 700 shares will be sold at that price by three different firms. According to the book, the quote and size on XYZ stock at this moment is:

81 1/4 – 81 5/8

16 by 7

The specialist has other orders to buy at lower prices and to sell at higher prices. He will use these orders to satisfy others who wish to buy and sell. For example, if a broker appears and wishes to buy 4,000 shares of XYZ, the specialist can provide 700 at 81 5/8, 2,900 at 81 3/4, and the remaining 400 at 81 7/8. At some point, the specialist could sell stock himself as principal, narrowing the price fluctuations further.

Are the orders on the book—to sell XYZ shares—short sales? That cannot be determined, as the sellers need not disclose this infor-

XYZ

500	ML		
700	MorganS		
1000	Janney MS		

1/8			
300	GoldmanS		
800	DeanWitter		
1500	Kidder P		

1/4			
100	AdvesT		
600	ML		
500	PruBache		
400	SalomonB		

3/8			

1/2			

5/8			

3/4			

7/8			

XYZ

1/8			

1/4			

3/8			

1/2			

5/8			
100	First Boston		
400	DillonRead		
200	ShearsonN		

3/4			
1000	Alex Brown		
1200	Smith Barny		
700	Bear Stearn		

7/8			
600	Lazard F.		
300	First Michigan		

Figure 5.1. Specialist's "book" showing orders for XYZ Company stock at prices ranging from $81 to $81 7/8 per share.

mation. They need only comply with the plus tick rule and make arrangements to borrow the stock for delivery to the buyer.

While the specialist's function as an agent contributes to the liquidity of the market, his role as a principal is far more important. It would be a simple matter to program the specialist's book into a computer; the book could be handled most efficiently in this manner. But when he acts as a principal, the specialist commits his firm's money. The transactions that he makes reduce the problems that would otherwise be caused by an imbalance of orders. If there are a large number of buyers or sellers for a particular stock, the orders on the book may not be sufficient to prevent wide price fluctuations. It is here that the specialist may step in to purchase or sell as principal, and thereby offset an imbalance that might otherwise distort the sequence of prices. In performing as principal, the specialist will frequently employ short sales. Specialists are not expected to prevent market movements. They are not, after all, working for charitable institutions; they are working for businesses. They are expected, however, to make positive contributions to the market's performance.

The specialist in XYZ stock is approached by a broker representing a large brokerage firm. The broker informs the specialist that he wishes to sell 10,000 shares of XYZ stock at the best price available. The buy orders on the specialist's book appear as follows:

		XYZ
1500	Prudential	51
1500	Dean Witter	51 1/8
1500	Paine Webber	51 1/4
2500	Morgan Stanley	51 3/8
1500	Goldman Sachs	51 1/2
500	Kidder Peabody	51 5/8
1000	Merrill Lynch	51 3/4

If the specialist executes the sell order solely against the buy orders on his book, he will make transactions at prices ranging from 51 3/4 down to 51. It will be necessary to go this far to find buyers for 10,000 shares. Suppose, however, that the specialist as principal is willing to purchase 3,000 shares at 51 1/4. He can now fill the order to sell without having the price drop below 51 1/4. This is not as radical as a decline to 51. The price still goes down, but not as sharply. The specialist now owns 3,000 shares of XYZ and may profit if the stock rises.

The specialist also sells as principal, and frequently these sales will be short sales. Because the price of ABD stock has been rising, not very many owners of the shares are willing to sell. The specialist can enter the market and sell for his own account, thereby accommodating the buyers. If he does not own any stock, the sales are all short sales. He sells short at continually rising prices, but he keeps these price changes orderly. In time the buying spree ends, investors begin to sell the stock, and the price is forced down. The specialist has a large short position and profits from the occurrence. There exists, of course, the inherent risk of being short, but in most cases the old axiom "What goes up must come down" applies, and the short sales by the specialist can be covered at a profit.

The specialist's short sales improved the market. He may also profit from the position. Unlike other investors, the specialist is not faced with transaction costs. If you sell short 100 shares of a stock at $60 a share, you may need a 1-point profit simply to cover your costs. If you cover your short at $59 a share, the $100 profit may barely pay the commissions you are charged on the two transactions. The specialist does not pay commissions. He may show a net gain on a profit of 1/4 point. As he trades in large volume, his per-share profits are multiplied and his earnings are comparably enhanced. Specialists can lose money when they act as principal; buying, selling long, or selling short carry risk. But specialists are professional market operators. Taking risks is the major component of their activity.

Short Selling Bonds

So far, our examples of short selling have been limited to stocks, but the practice is also common in the trading of bonds.

A client, perhaps a large pension fund, calls a brokerage firm that deals in corporate bonds. The pension fund wishes to sell $1 million in AT&T bonds with an interest rate of 8 3/8 percent and a maturity date in the year 2007. The brokerage firm is ecstatic. It has another client, a savings bank, interested in purchasing these bonds. The firm will buy from the pension fund, sell to the savings bank, and show a profit for its efforts.

There is, however, a catch. With the money raised by the sale of the AT&T bonds, the pension fund wants to purchase $1 million of Cleveland Electric bonds with a 9 1/4 percent interest rate and a maturity date in the year 2009. But try as it may, the brokerage firm can find only $900,000 of the Cleveland bonds available for sale. Would the firm lose the entire trade over this comparatively trivial amount? Of course it won't. It will short the additional $100,000 of Cleveland Electric and complete the trade. They will cover the short later in order to profit from today's activities. There is a risk, of course, but this is the firm's business. By selling short, it has completed transactions that otherwise would not have been possible.

Arbitrage and Short Selling

Another area of the market that frequently employs short selling is arbitrage. The term *arbitrage* can best be defined as the near-simultaneous purchase and sale of the same or exchangeable securities in the hope of attaining a profit through a difference in markets. Put simply, the arbitrageur tries to find a situation in which he can buy at one price and sell at a higher price at virtually the same time. There are many ways that the arbitrage technique can be employed. In most cases, a short sale is part of the device. Consider the following examples.

The simplest form of arbitrage deals in geographic differences in security prices. Suppose a trader in New York notes that CBS stock is trading on the New York Stock Exchange at $182 a share. By consulting his quotation monitor, he finds the same stock price at $180 a share on the Pacific Stock Exchange. He quickly sells in New York and buys in California, recording a profit of $2 a share. The sale in New York is technically a short sale, but he will deliver the shares that he purchased when settlement occurs.

Arbitrage frequently uses exchangeable securities, such as *preemptive rights, options,* or convertible bonds and preferred *stock.*

A preemptive right is a privilege given to stockholders to purchase additional shares at a fixed price called the subscription price.

If the true value of the rights is higher than the market price, an arbitrage might be possible.

For example, MNO Corporation is offering its holders the right to purchase additional stock at a subscription price of $50 a share. Under the terms of the offering, a person must submit 4 rights and $50 to purchase each new share. Both the stock and the rights are trading in the market. The price of the stock is $56 a share. Compute the true value of each right. To start, find the value of the premium:

$$
\begin{array}{ll}
\$56 & \text{Market price} \\
\underline{\$50} & \text{Subscription price} \\
\$\ 6 & \text{Premium}
\end{array}
$$

The premium is the amount by which the market price of the stock exceeds the subscription price. A person who subscribes to stock at $50 will have an immediate profit of $6 a share.

Since it requires 4 rights to purchase each share at $50 the rights should be worth $1.50 each:

$$
\frac{6.00}{4} \ \frac{\text{Premium}}{\text{Rights}} = \$1.50 \text{ per right}
$$

Suppose a trader finds the rights available at $1 each. He executes an arbitrage by purchasing 4 rights at $1 and simultaneously selling 1 share of MNO Corporation stock short at $56 a share. With the 4 rights that cost him a total of $4, he subscribes to 1 new share by paying $50. Total cost for the new share is $54, but he has already sold the share at $56. The $2 per-share profit is his to spend.

Arbitrage is often practiced using convertible securities. For example, LDC Corporation has outstanding 9 percent debentures, which are convertible into LDC common stock at $25 a share. Since a bond has a face value of $1,000, this means that each bond can be exchanged for 40 shares of the common stock:

$$
\frac{\$1,000}{\$25} \ \frac{\text{Face value}}{\text{Conversion price}} = 40 \text{ shares}
$$

The arbitrageur will compute a figure known as *parity*—the price at which the stock and bond are equal (or at "parity")—and he will wait for an opportunity to move if these prices get out of line. For example, if the market price of the stock is $22, to be at parity the bond must be $880. As each bond is equivalent to 40 shares of stock, the bond price at parity is 40 times the price of the stock.

Suppose the bond price was $1,240. Parity for the stock would be $31 a share. Since each bond can be exchanged for 40 shares of stock, the bond price ($1,240) is divided by 40 to arrive at parity for the stock.

Some samples of parity for these securities are as follows:

Common Stock	Bond
20	$ 800
28	$1,120
34	$1,360
40	$1,600

In each case, the bond price is 40 times the stock price and the stock price is 1/40 of the bond price.

Suppose the LDC Corporation bond is actually trading at $1,600 (a price of 160) and the stock is at $42 a share. The trader moves quickly, purchasing one bond for $1,600 and selling 40 shares of stock short at $42 a share. The proceeds of this sale bring him $1,680 ($42 × 40 shares) for an immediate gross profit of $80. By purchasing the bond at $1,600, he is actually purchasing the stock at $40 a share; by selling at $42, he pockets the profit.

The sale of the stock in this example is called a *short exempt* transaction. It is a short sale, as the arbitrageur does not own the stock. Because he owns the convertible bond, which enables him to make delivery without borrowing shares, the trade is exempt from the plus tick rule that was discussed previously.

Needless to say, the opportunities to engage in a bona fide arbitrage are quite few. The term implies an immediate profit, and that is not easily found in any business. With the large number of astute traders operating in today's markets, any disparity between markets will be quickly closed. Executing a true arbitrage is similar to finding a $100 bill on the sidewalk. When is the last time that happened to you?

Risk Arbitrage

A situation more likely to occur than an arbitrage is a risk arbitrage. As the term implies, the profit is not guaranteed, and the maneuver may well result in substantial loss. Again, selling short frequently plays a part in this practice and is worth examination.

The Mammoth Oil Company has announced its plans to acquire all of the stock of the Medium Oil Corporation. Both companies have agreed to the terms of the deal. For every 2 shares of Medium Oil, the holders will receive 1 share of Mammoth Oil. The prices of the two stocks in the market are as follows:

Mammoth Oil	$42
Medium Oil	$18

The arbitrageur makes her move. She purchases 2 shares of Medium at $18 (total cost, $36) and sells 1 share of Mammoth short at $42. When she receives the 2 Medium shares, she will exchange them for 1 share of Mammoth. She will then deliver this share to complete her short sale and enjoy the $6 profit that resulted.

But this is a risk arbitrage. Two weeks after our trader made her apparent coup, the U.S. Government is heard from. The Justice Department denies the two companies the right to merge, as the merger would be considered to be in restraint of trade. With the merger now called off, Medium stock drops to $12 and Mammoth stock quickly rises to $55. Our risk arbitrageur is now losing in both directions. The Medium stock that she purchased is down 6 points, and the Mammoth stock that she sold short is up 13 points.

Not all risk arbitrage results in the losses demonstrated in this example, but such a situation is possible. Although this example is fictitious, a very similar situation occurred some years ago when a proposed merger between Gulf Oil and Cities Service was stopped by the government.

The short sales examined so far all have a common characteristic: the seller was selling a security that he or she did not own. In the case of the short exempt sale, an exchangeable security was owned but it was not the exact item sold.

Selling Short against the Box

In some cases, a short seller actually owns the security he is selling but does not plan to deliver it to the purchaser. This type of short sale is called short against the box, or short versus box. The seller owns the stock but leaves it in his safe deposit box. Instead, he delivers borrowed stock. Short sales against the box are considered to be short sales in all aspects and must adhere to the plus tick requirement.

There are two principal reasons for employing a short versus box sale. The first is to allow an investor to take advantage of a temporary decline in the value of a stock she owns without losing her position.

Some years ago, a client purchased Teledyne stock at $4 a share. This has proved to be a wise move, as Teledyne is now trading at $40 a share. The client feels that in the current market the shares should decline in price perhaps to $35 a share. She does not want to sell the stock she bought at $4, as her analysis tells her that this decline will be temporary. In time Teledyne will resume its upward movement, and her profit will increase. Additionally, she does not wish to assume the tax liability that will accrue if she sells her stock and creates a large capital gain. So she sells her stock short versus box.

The client enters the order, and her broker sells the stock short at $40 a share. Her broker arranges to borrow the shares for her, and they are delivered according to the terms of the contract. She is now long and short the same number of Teledyne shares, giving her an even position. If Teledyne declines to $35, she may repurchase the shares that she sold short. She will have a profit on this short sale and will have retained her long position. Naturally, she has a paper loss of 5 points on her long position, but this is offset by the profit she made. Had she not sold short versus box, she would have the loss in her holdings with no compensating gain.

A short versus box sale can have the effect of protecting a long position in periods of temporary market decline.

As always, however, there is risk. Suppose after selling short against the box at $40 the client watches as Teledyne stock goes up instead of down. It rises to $45, then $50, then perhaps $60. While her original holding is showing a profit, she has a corresponding loss in her short position. If she had only left things alone and not sold short, she would have benefited from the price increases. If the price keeps rising, she may even be forced to take the stock out of the box to return to the lender and cover the short. In this case she has no position left in Teledyne, and her earlier short sale at $40 becomes the price at which she disposed of her long position. If one sells short against the box, one is not subject to the unlimited loss that faces the usual short seller. The short seller is, however, liable for any dividends paid on the borrowed stock; thus, a short sale against the box is not without cost. On the other hand, if things go against the client, she does have the stock and can make delivery. But the result will not be to her liking.

The short versus box technique can also be used in a manner that has nothing to do with speculating in the market. This is an often useful application that can improve one's tax situation by permitting a person to defer a capital gain from one year to another. It does not eliminate the tax, but does allow for a postponement in the payment schedule.

A client has a substantial profit in XYZ stock. He purchased 1,000 shares many years ago at $10 a share, and today the price is $90 a share. He would like to sell and take his profit, but he is not anxious to pay the tax on the gain in this tax year. Perhaps he has taken other substantial gains this year and would prefer to push this one forward to next year. But he fears that if he waits until next January, the market may decline and his profit will be reduced.

Another possibility is that he plans to retire at the year's end. How nice it would be to defer this gain to the following year, when his income and resulting tax bracket will be lower. If he waits until January, the market might reclaim a major part of his profit. Using a short versus box sale, the client can have the best of both worlds. He can sell the stock this year and avoid assuming liability for the tax until next year. In early November he enters the following order:

Sell	1000	XYZ	Market	Short

The firm handling the order is aware that the sale is short versus box, but the broker handling the order on the Exchange floor need only be told that it is short. The broker's only concern is adherence to the plus tick rule which applies to short versus box sales as well as to regular short sales.

The stock is sold short at $90, and the client has locked in his profit of $80 a share. Through his broker, he borrows the 1,000 shares and makes delivery. His actual position in XYZ is zero. He has 1,000 shares in the box, but he is short an equal amount. He cannot be hurt by any market decline as he is both long and short. It also follows that he will not participate in any rise in XYZ's price, but this was not his consideration. He wanted to get out of the stock and postpone the tax bite.

On the first business day of the following January, his broker removes the stock from the client's account and returns it to the original lender. At that point, the transaction is completed, and the gain becomes taxable. The client sold the stock in November but was not liable for the tax until January of the following year. This can be a most-useful device for many clients with unique tax situations.

The uses of short selling are many and varied. The technique is employed to speculate, to hedge positions, to facilitate other transactions, and to accrue tax benefits. Additional short-selling strategies are initiated by using options and futures, which will be discussed later.

Short Selling a New Issue

Investment bankers often find the short sale a valuable tool in ensuring the success of a new issue of stock. A large group of investment bankers (called a syndicate) is planning to offer 1 million shares of Happy Days Fashion Corporation stock to the public next week. This is the initial public offering for these shares; no market for the stock currently exists. The syndicate manager, perhaps Morgan Stanley & Co., keeps a close watch on the progress of the deal.

While the members of the syndicate cannot actually sell the shares until released to do so by the SEC, they are permitted to contact their clients to predetermine their interest in the offering. Large institutions contact the manager directly to indicate their interest in buying some Happy Days stock. A day or so prior to the official offering date, Morgan Stanley feels that the interest has not yet been as great as the firm had hoped. When the shares are offered at $10 each and begin to trade in the open market, the price might drop. If all of the shares are not sold, some of the purchasers might elect to sell out immediately, leading to a decline.

To combat this possibility, Morgan Stanley may sell some stock short. The firm will cause more than 1 million shares to be distributed by filling orders with stock it does not have. If a large financial institution calls and requests 10,000 shares, Morgan Stanley will sell the stock to the institution even though the firm does not have it. By doing this, the firm builds up a short position. When the stock begins trading in the market, Morgan Stanley must purchase shares to cover the short. This process, called *overallotting*, gives support to the market and perhaps even prevents a decline in price.

Obviously, there is risk involved. If Morgan Stanley sells stock short at $10 and has to pay a higher price to repurchase it, a loss will result. But these bankers are professionals and know their business. In addition, any loss will be shared proportionately by all members of the syndicate. This process often results in a successful deal that otherwise might not have been possible. The short sale was a positive contribution to the offering. The risk involved is a small price to pay.

No matter what the purpose of selling short, the most important element is the ability to borrow the shares. The mechanics of short selling are just as important as the applications.

6

The Mechanics of Selling Short

If you wish to open an account with a brokerage firm for the purposes of buying and selling securities, that firm is required to make a thorough investigation of your personal and financial status. The information required may vary from firm to firm, but it is the firm's responsibility to evaluate what is suitable for each client.

The information the firm gathers is then recorded in a document known as a *new account form*.

While the firm is permitted to request whatever data it finds appropriate, at the minimum the following facts should be disclosed:

Customer's name

Home address

Home phone number

Business address

Business phone number

Type of business

Position

Aproximate income

Approximate net worth

Bank references

Taxpayer's ID number

Previous investment
   experience

Approximate age

Citizenship

Investment objective

Type of account (cash or
   margin)

The information is then studied by a principal of the firm. If he is satisfied that the data are sufficient, the account is approved for trading. The approval may include some restrictions on the types of trades the client may enter into. For example, if the client is retired and has stated an objective of safety of principal and income, the firm would be unlikely to allow the client to engage in speculative market practices. In this example, selling short would not be at all appropriate. The principal determination in handling customer's accounts is suitability. The concept is often elusive, as it includes both financial and emotional considerations. But brokerage firms must exert great effort to see that recommendations made to a client are suitable to that investor's financial objectives.

THE MARGIN ACCOUNT

If the client plans only to buy and sell securities long, she may choose to open either a cash or a margin account. But if she contemplates selling securities short, she must maintain a *margin account* for this purpose. All short sales must be made in margin accounts.

As the term indicates, a cash account requires the client to make full payment for any securities purchased. If she buys 200 shares of AT&T at a total cost of $8,250, she must deposit the full amount. If she later sells these shares long, her cash account is credited with the proceeds of the sale. But when a client sells short, the cost of the purchase cannot be determined because she has not as yet bought anything. Later she will cover the short, but at this point it is not known when or at what cost. Since a short sale results in an open transaction, all such trades must be executed in a margin account.

RULES FOR PURCHASING SECURITIES

Before studying the mechanics of short selling, the general rules for purchasing securities in a margin account must be understood. These rules are set down by the Federal Reserve Board under Regulation T ("Reg T"), which governs brokers who handle margin transactions for clients. A similar Federal Reserve rule (Regulation U) governs banks in the margin area.

Reg T sets the minimum amount that a client must deposit when purchasing securities on margin. The example below assumes that this margin requirement is 50 percent.

Mary Jones opens a new account at Dean Witter & Co. and purchases the following securities:

100 AT&T	$ 4,000
200 GM	8,000
100 IBM	12,000

As the total cost of the three purchases is $24,000, Ms. Jones must deposit a minimum of $12,000. But the securities cost $24,000; where does the remaining $12,000 come from? She borrows the money from her broker, Dean Witter. After the transactions are completed, her account appears as follows:

Market value	$24,000
Debt balance	12,000
Equity	12,000

If you purchased a house for $24,000 (not very likely in today's market), put up $12,000 of your own money, and took a mortgage for $12,000 from the local bank, it would be exactly the same situation (market value = $24,000; mortgage (debit) = $12,000; equity = $12,000).

The broker may obtain the money that he lends Mary Jones by arranging for a *call-loan* from a bank. As collateral, Dean Witter pledges to the bank some of the securities in Ms. Jones's account. She has already pledged her securities to Dean Witter. On Wall Street it is not fashionable to use a simple word like pledge when a more confusing one is available, so the term used is *hypothocation*. Mary Jones hypothocates the securities to Dean Witter, which then rehypothocates them to the bank. Naturally, the bank charges interest to Dean Witter on the loan, perhaps 10 percent, but Dean Witter charges interest to Ms. Jones, perhaps 15 percent. The amount of interest charged will vary, depending on the size of the loan and the amount of commissions that the client generates through her trading.

In some cases, Dean Witter may raise the money for the loan by lending the client's securities to other customers—or even to other firms. This is usually done to allow the party to make short sales.

Where does Dean Witter obtain the right to pledge Ms. Jones's securities at the bank or to lend them to other people? She gave the firm this privilege when she opened the account. A person who opens a margin account signs two documents: the *customer's agreement* and the *customer's loan consent*.

In the customer's agreement, often called the margin agreement, the client permits the use of her securities as collateral for a bank loan. In the customer's loan consent, she allows the brokerage firm to lend her securities to others. As you will see, this can be very profitable for the brokerage firm.

Figure 6.1 shows a portion of a customer's agreement and a customer's loan consent. In the customer's agreement, which the client signs, note item 5. This is the paragraph that permits the pledging of the client's stock at the bank. The customer's loan consent is very brief and general, but it gives the broker the right "to lend to yourselves as brokers or to others, any securities held by you on margin for the account of or under the control of the undersigned."

If the value of Ms. Jones's securities rises, her equity will rise in tandem. If the market value declines, her equity will follow. If the equity declines to a degree that might endanger the broker, she may be required to deposit additional funds or securities to provide additional protection for the broker. The regulations are established by the firms handling the account and by the New York Stock Exchange. If the client receives a request for additional funds (known as a *margin call*) and does not respond, the firm may liquidate the securities held in her account. (See item 4 in the customer's agreement.)

THE SHORT SELLING PROCESS

The conditions of Reg T apply to short sellers just as they do to purchasers. If you sell securities short, you must deposit a mini-

CUSTOMER'S AGREEMENT

JANNEY MONTGOMERY SCOTT INC.

Gentlemen:

In consideration of your accepting one or more accounts of the undersigned (whether designated by name, number or otherwise) and your agreeing to act as brokers for the undersigned in the purchase or sale of securities or commodities, the undersigned agrees as follows:

1. That all transactions between us shall be subject to the rules and customs of the market or exchange (and its Clearing House, if any) where executed. You may employ sub-brokers and shall be responsible only for reasonable care in their selection.

2. Whenever any statute shall be enacted which shall affect in any manner or be inconsistent with any of the provisions hereof or whenever any rule or regulation shall be prescribed or promulgated by the New York Stock Exchange, the Federal Securities and Exchange Commission, the Board of Governors of the Federal Reserve System and/or the Secretary of Agriculture which shall affect in any manner or be inconsistent with any of the provisions hereof, the provisions of this agreement so affected shall be deemed modified or superseded, as the case may be, by such statue, rule or regulation, and all other provisions of the agreement and the provisions as so modified or superseded, shall in all respects continue to be in full force and effect.

3. Except as herein otherwise expressly provided, no provision of this agreement shall in any respect be waived, altered, modified or amended unless such waiver, alteration, modification or amendment be committed to writing and signed by a member of your organization.

4. All monies, securities, commodities or other property which you may at any time be carrying for the undersigned or which may at any time be in your possession for any purpose, including safekeeping, shall be subject to a general lien for the discharge of all obligations of the undersigned to you, irrespective of whether or not you have made advances in connection with such securities, commodities or other property, and irrespective of the number of accounts the undersigned may have with you.

5. That all liability of the undersigned to you shall be secured by all stocks and/or securities of the undersigned held by you, and you are hereby authorized without having in your possession or subject to your control other stocks and/or securities of the same kind and amount, and without notice to the undersigned, to loan and repledge the same (either for the amount due from the undersigned or for a greater sum), from time to time, separately or together with other stocks and/or securities.

6. That you may charge monthly, as interest or otherwise, such sums to compensate you for advances made on my account at the prevailing and/or allowable rates according to the laws of the State of New York, as you may determine upon acceptance of the agreement and thereafter.

CUSTOMER'S LOAN CONSENT

Until you receive written notice of revocation from the undersigned, you are hereby authorized to lend, to yourselves as brokers or to others, any securities held by you on margin for the account of, or under the control of, the undersigned.

Dated _____   Signature _____

_____

ACCEPTED _____
                      JANNEY MONTGOMERY SCOTT INC.

Figure 6.1. Part of the typical Customer's Agreement with a brokerage firm, including the Customer's Loan Consent. (Copyright Janney Montgomery Scott Inc. Reproduced by permission.)

mum of 50 percent of the proceeds of the sale. This requirement serves two purposes. First, it protects the broker, should the stock rise in value. If the firm is required to purchase the shares at a price higher than the short sale, there will be a loss. If the client disappears, the broker will sustain this loss. The 50 percent deposit provides the broker with protection. Second, when you sell stock short, you effectively create the shares. If you sell 100 shares of IBM short, the stock must be borrowed for delivery to the buyer. Hence, there are two owners of the same 100 shares, the lender of the stock and the purchaser. Since in a sense you created the second 100 shares, your deposit in part offsets the existence of this additional value. It is part of the Federal Reserve's function to control the amount of money and credit in our economy.

For example, a new client of Janney Montgomery Scott & Co., Mr. Charles Kaplan, wishes to sell 1,000 shares of CBS stock short.

Mr. Kaplan has signed all the necessary documents, and Janney Montgomery Scott has determined that its client is financially and emotionally able to assume the risk involved.

Prior to entering the order, Janney Montgomery Scott must ascertain its ability to borrow the shares. Perhaps the firm could borrow the shares from the accounts of some of its other clients who have signed the customer's loan consent. If the firm cannot borrow in this manner, it will attempt to borrow the stock from other firms. Merrill Lynch may agree to lend the stock by taking it from the accounts of clients who own CBS shares and have signed the customer's loan consent.

Janney Montgomery Scott now places the following order on the floor of the New York Stock Exchange:

Sell	1000	CBS	Market	Short

The firm's broker goes to the post and sells the stock at $180 a share. Naturally, the sale conforms to the plus tick requirement. Perhaps the buyer of the stock is Goldman Sachs & Co. As the proceeds of the sale are $180,000, under Reg T Mr. Kaplan must deposit 50 percent, or $90,000.

On settlement date for the trade, Merrill Lynch lends 1,000 shares of CBS to Janney Montgomery Scott, which delivers it to the purchaser Goldman Sachs. Goldman Sachs pays Janney Montgomery Scott $180,000, which Janney Montgomery Scott then delivers to Merrill Lynch as security for the loan of the stock. Figure 6.2 illustrates the transaction.

When the delivery and settlement are accomplished, the position of the three parties involved will be as follows:

1. *Goldman Sachs*   Purchased 1,000 shares of CBS, received the shares from Janney Montgomery Scott, and paid the agreed amount of $180,000.

2. *Merrill Lynch*   Loaned Janney Montgomery Scott 1,000 shares of CBS, which it took from the accounts of Merrill Lynch clients who had given written permission to do so. As collateral it received $180,000 in cash.

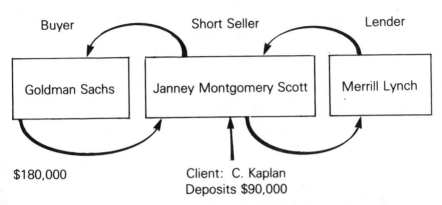

Figure 6.2. Short sale of 1,000 shares of CBS stock at $180 per share.

3. *Janney Montgomery Scott* Received the 1,000 shares on loan from Merrill Lynch, but delivered them to Goldman Sachs. Janney Montgomery Scott received $180,000 from Goldman Sachs, but delivered it to Merrill Lynch as security. The firm does not have the stock or the sale proceeds, but it does have a deposit of $90,000 from its client.

Goldman Sachs has no further part in this transaction. The firm received what it purchased and paid for it. Merrill Lynch has loaned the stock from its customers' accounts, but has received the world's best collateral—cash. Janney Montgomery Scott is carrying the short position for Mr. Kaplan, but has his $90,000 deposit as protection against loss. The firm also receives a commission from the client for executing his order. (The commission is not considered in these calculations, but it would be a factor in an actual trade.)

At some point in the future, Mr. Kaplan will cover his short. Assume that he later buys the shares at $160 each. He pays $160,000 (plus commission), and when the stock is received he returns it to Merrill Lynch. Since he made his sale for $180,000, he will have a profit of $20,000 less expenses. Of course, he may not be so fortunate. If he covered the short at $200 a share (for a total cost of $200,000), he would show a loss of $20,000 plus expenses.

After the original short sale was made at $180 a share, the client's margin account contained the following information:

$180,000	Sale proceeds
+ 90,000	Margin deposit
$270,000	Credit balance
− 180,000	Current market value
$ 90,000	Adjusted credit balance (equity)

As the price of CBS stock rises or falls, the new market value will be subtracted from the $270,000 credit balance. Thus, if the stock rises, the client's equity declines. For example, the market price rises to $190:

$180,000	Sale proceeds
+ 90,000	Margin deposit
$270,000	Credit balance
− 190,000	Current market value
$ 80,000	Adjusted credit balance (equity)

If the value of CBS stock declines, the client's equity increases. For example, the market price declines to $150,000:

$180,000	Sale proceeds
+ 90,000	Margin deposit
$270,000	Credit balance
− 150,000	Current market value
$120,000	Adjusted credit balance (equity)

Short Selling and the Broker

To accomplish this short sale, the one necessary element was the ability to borrow 1,000 shares of CBS stock. In this hypothetical situation, Janney Montgomery Scott did not have the shares available but was able to borrow them from Merrill Lynch.

Why would Merrill Lynch be willing to lend this stock and assist a competitive firm? The answer, quite simply, is to make money. Remember, Merrill Lynch did not lend its own stock; the firm obtained stock from the accounts of clients who had signed the customer's loan consent. But on delivery of the stock, the firm received $180,000 from Janney Montgomery Scott that Merrill Lynch could use to conduct its own business. Perhaps Merrill Lynch could lend the money to other clients who had purchased stock on margin and had a debit balance, such as Mary Jones in the example given earlier. Merrill Lynch could lend Ms. Jones and others the money received on the loan of the CBS stock and still charge interest. There would be no need to go to the bank and make a call loan on which the firm must pay interest; the firm would use the money it received at no cost. Any interest charged would be income to the firm.

It is interesting to study the annual reports of large brokerage firms that have a large supply of stock available to lend. In periods of high interest rates, the income received from this lending process is often one of their largest sources of revenue. It is a marvelous situation. Using someone else's securities as collateral, they borrow money and pay no interest. They then lend this money to others and charge them the going interest rate. It is hard to conceive of a more desirable situation.

Do not forget the firm that handled the account of the short seller. It received a $90,000 deposit from the client, which it might use by lending to other clients and charging interest.

Short sellers do wonderful things for brokerage firms. They create a vast pool of funds that become available for loans. If a short seller is a very active trader, he will be aware of this and may request a share of the profits. He might ask for interest on his equity as a reward for his good work. After all, it is the short seller, not the broker, who assumes the risk. He may expect to share in the rewards.

The lending of stock has become a major profit center for many major brokerage firms. Since these firms maintain a large number of accounts for clients, they have a huge supply of stock available for lending; and since the cash received in return for the stock can be employed to create interest, the firms actively seek out borrowers of shares. These firms maintain a stock loan department that will contact other firms and offer to supply their needs.

Some firms also act as middlemen for those seeking to borrow stock. These firms, known as finders, assist brokers in locating needed shares. Because this area of the securities industry is not widely understood, the professionals who utilize it can often profit handsomely. In cases involving big money, scandals often follow. Since the 1980s, a number of Wall Street people have been indicted for crimes resulting from the stock loan business. The violations included misuse of the funds created as well as improper, unreported payments to suppliers and borrowers of stock in order to receive favorable treatment.

When client Kaplan sold the 1,000 shares of CBS stock short at $180 a share, his broker, Janney Montgomery Scott, borrowed the shares from Merrill Lynch and delivered them to the buyer, Goldman Sachs. It would seem that nothing further will occur until Mr. Kaplan decides to cover his short, but this is not at all the case.

It is important to consider the rights of the Merrill Lynch clients whose shares were used to facilitate this loan. Remember that those shares were delivered to Goldman Sachs and have no doubt been transferred to the name of the Goldman Sachs client who ordered the purchase. Therefore, although the Merrill Lynch clients own the shares and the ownership will be shown on their monthly account statements, the shares are in fact gone. Do they know about this? Probably not. The broker who lends the stock is not obligated to inform the owners. They have given written permission for this action to be taken.

So an odd position is reached. Two clients own the same 1,000 shares of CBS—the Merrill Lynch clients and the Goldman Sachs client. But the CBS corporation recognizes only one owner on its records—Goldman Sachs. When CBS takes any action regarding its stockholders, such as payment of a dividend, it deals with the registered owner—the Goldman Sach's client.

What about the lenders from Merrill Lynch? Have they lost their rights as stockholders? Have they been disenfranchised? Not at all. The second 1,000 shares of CBS stock, which is not recognized by the company, was actually created by the short seller. As all of us, particularly parents, know, when you create something you support it. The short seller will support his child—1,000 shares of CBS—in proper fashion.

RIGHTS AND OBLIGATIONS

Many questions must be answered regarding the rights of the lenders of stock and the corresponding obligations of the short seller:

What if the shares of CBS rise in value?

What if the lenders wish to sell these shares?

What if CBS pays a cash dividend?

What if CBS pays a stock dividend?

What if CBS splits its stock?

What about the lender's right to vote?

In all cases except one—that of voting rights—the lender is protected. This protection is the duty of the short seller.

Shortly after the transaction is made, CBS stock rises to $200 a share. The 1,000 shares now have a market value of $200,000. The short seller provided the lender with only $180,000. In this case, the lender can send to the borrower a request called a *mark to market*. This procedure requires the borrower to increase the collateral to an amount equal to the current value of the stock. The short seller's broker, Janney Montgomery Scott, will deliver $20,000 to Merrill Lynch. This amount will be charged to the client's account, thereby reducing his equity. The lenders are now secure since, in the event the borrower fails to return their shares, Merrill Lynch now has sufficient funds to replace them. Marking to market is a two-way street. If the shares declined in value to $160, the borrower could request the return of $20,000. However, this would still leave an amount equivalent to the market value as collateral.

Two weeks after this transaction is completed, a Merrill Lynch client calls and orders that her shares be sold. She may not know that her physical stock has been loaned, but this does not affect the situation. Merrill Lynch sells her shares as ordered, then contacts the borrower, Janney Montgomery Scott, and demands return of the shares. Because Janney Montgomery Scott does not have the stock, it must find a new lender. Perhaps Paine Webber agrees to lend the shares. When the shares are received, they are returned to Merrill Lynch, which in turn returns the money. The money is now transferred to Paine Webber as security. But suppose that Janney Montgomery Scott cannot locate another lender. In that case the firm is forced to buy the shares and cover the short for return to the lender. Since most transactions to purchase or sell securities allow five business days for settlement, that same period is given to the borrower to locate a new lender or to cover the short.

In the month following the short sale, CBS declares a dividend of $1.10 a share to the holders of its common stock. Thus, the holder of 1,000 shares, including the lenders at Merrill Lynch, can expect to receive $1,100 on the payment date. CBS, however, will not send them any money at all. According to CBS's records, the Goldman Sachs client gets the check. Who pays Merrill Lynch? Correct, the short seller. On payment date of the dividend, Janney Montgomery Scott sends Merrill Lynch a check for $1,100, which it charges to the account of the short seller. Merrill Lynch credits the money to the accounts of the lenders. They have received what they were due in full.

This situation illustrates another danger inherent in selling stock short. The buyer of stock pays for it and puts it away. If the stock goes down, he is not pleased but he is not required to deposit any more money. Even if the value is lower, he might still receive a dividend check every three months to soften the blow. Not so with the short seller. If the stock rises, he may have to come up with additional funds. If the point is reached where he has no more funds, he will be forced to cover the short, probably at the most inopportune moment. In addition, during the period in which he is short, his account is charged for any dividends declared by the company. This also depletes his funds. But he is supporting his creation—1,000 shares of CBS stock.

Suppose CBS declares a 10 percent stock dividend. When this occurs, all shareholders are given additional shares equal to 10 percent of their holdings. The lenders at Merrill Lynch are entitled to 100 shares as their 10 percent dividend on the 1,000 shares owned. Where do they come from? The short seller, of course. He must borrow another 100 shares of CBS and deliver to Merrill Lynch. A stock dividend generally causes a decline in the market value of the shares. Therefore, the value of the 1,100 shares now borrowed will probably not exceed the value of the 1,000 shares prior to the dividend, and no additional cash collateral will be necessary.

Stock splits are treated in the same manner as stock dividends. If CBS splits its stock 2 for 1, each holder will have his or her number of shares doubled. The owners of 1,000 shares would now own 2,000 shares, and the short seller would have to borrow the additional stock for delivery to the lender. But since the price of the stock would also decline to reflect the split, note that the value would be roughly the same:

1,000 shares of CBS × $180 a share = $180,000
2,000 shares of CBS × $ 90 a share = $180,000

The only privilege of common stock ownership that the lender actually loses is the right to vote. When CBS holds its annual meeting, all common stockholders are entitled to vote on all matters before the meeting. If stockholders are unable to attend the meeting in person, they are sent an absentee ballot called a *proxy*. Despite the fact that the 1,000 shares are owned by two different people, CBS will permit only the registered owner of the stock to vote. While the short seller can provide cash dividends, stock dividends, and stock splits to the lender, he cannot create 1,000 votes at the meeting. Therefore the lender loses the right to vote. Most, but not all, corporate meetings are routine, however, and the loss of voting rights is seldom critical. Most stockholders never even bother to vote their stock unless something momentous, such as a merger or a takeover, is in question. The lender nonetheless loses the voting privilege. He is not given the option of exercising or not exercising this inherent right.

FEES AND COMPLICATIONS

We have seen how the mechanics of short selling are handled. There are still other possible complications.

If a stock is in short supply, it will be difficult to borrow. For example, perhaps a particular stock is the subject of merger rumors and has risen greatly in price. This might bring a number of short sellers into the market who feel that the price increase has been overdone and that a decline may be imminent. This excess of short sellers who must borrow shares may greatly diminish the amount of stock available for loan. In these cases the short seller may be required to pay a fee for the use of the stock. The fee, called the premium, is based on dollars per day paid for each 100 shares borrowed, and is negotiated between the parties involved. For example, if XYZ stock is in short supply, a short seller wishing to borrow 1,000 shares may have to pay a premium of $2 per hundred. This means that for each business day he uses the borrowed stock, he will pay the lending firm $20. This is an additional cost for the short seller, as his account is already charged with the premium. In reality, premiums for borrowing stock are quite rare. In recent years, they have seldom occurred and then only in the most unusual circumstances.

Another fee sometimes connected with a stock loan is known as *lending at a rate*. This refers to the payment of a rate of interest to the borrower of the stock by the lender. In the CBS example the short seller's broker, Janney Montgomery Scott, delivered $180,000 to Merrill Lynch to secure the loan on the stock. Perhaps current interest rates would permit Merrill Lynch to lend this money at 15 percent interest. Janney Montgomery Scott may therefore request a rate of interest, perhaps 5 percent, on the $180,000. This payment of a rate may influence a borrower's decision in determining from whom he should borrow the stock.

If stock lends at a premium or at a rate, will the money earned be credited to the actual client? Will the premium be credited to the account of the person lending the stock? Will the rate of interest be credited to the client who actually sold the stock short? It is safe to say that in most cases the answer is no. The brokerage firm usually retains these fees. But a knowledgeable client who has a substantial account should become informed of his broker's policy in these matters. He may be able to enhance his own return by demanding a share.

In fact, most loans of stock are made flat, which means that there is no premium to borrow and no rate of interest to lend. Firms assist each other to build reciprocal arrangements. You may lend stock to a firm today and borrow some other item from the firm tomorrow. If there were no lending of stock, there could be no short selling. Recognizing this fact, dealers generally strive to accommodate their competitors.

An examination of the process of short selling reveals that more people are involved than it would seem at first. Many of them do not even realize that they are part of the strategy. A client may have a margin account at a firm, which she uses only to purchase stocks and bonds. Never would she consider selling short. But if she has signed the customer's loan consent—and most likely she has—her precious securities may now be in the possession of some other person. Were it not for her, that party may not have been able to complete his short sale. She is a player in the game, although she may not be aware of it.

This is not to suggest that clients should refuse to allow their securities to be loaned. It has already been shown that short sellers add liquidity to the market. Their actions provide benefits for the more conservative investors by creating more favorable prices when the short sellers sell short and when they cover their positions.

Lenders have adequate protection since their broker receives the cash value of the stock loaned. In the event of a brokerage firm's failing, the Securities Investor Protection Corporation (SIPC) provides up to $500,000 insurance for each customer. Many brokerage firms carry additional insurance to further protect their clients.

You do not have to be a short seller yourself to participate in the process. You may never gamble, but you might very much enjoy the thrills and pageantry of the Kentucky Derby.

7
Protecting Short Positions: Equity Options

Every investment entails some degree of risk. Even the most conservative position—with U.S. Treasury securities—presents some danger of loss. Because short selling can bring with it unlimited risk, this chapter discusses devices that short sellers can employ to minimize these risks.

STOP ORDERS

Suppose a client sells 100 shares of General Electric short at $70 a share. He feels that these shares will decline in value and that he will be able to cover the short at a profit. If he is wrong, his loss can be unlimited. To protect himself, he can utilize a unique type of order called a *buy stop order.*

Three types of orders are employed in securities transactions—*market orders, limit orders,* and *stop orders.* A market order simply instructs the client's broker to buy or sell at the best price available. Should you wish to purchase shares of IBM and are not concerned about the price, you would enter the following order:

Buy   100   IBM   Market

The firm handling your business would direct your order to the floor of the New York Stock Exchange, where its representative would buy the stock at the then-current price. Perhaps the client would be informed that the shares had been purchased at $116 a share.

In contrast, a limit order sets a specific price limitation. The client may be unwilling to pay more than $115 a share for IBM, so the following order would be entered:

Buy   100   IBM   115

This order instructs the broker to pay no more than $115 a share for the stock. Naturally, if the price does not decline to that figure, the shares will not be purchased. But the client is adamant. He will go no higher than 115.

Market and limit orders are quite simple to understand; stop orders are a bit more complicated. A stop order represents a memorandum order containing a price that becomes a market order when that price is reached or surpassed. In some ways, stop orders are the direct opposite of limit orders. A buy limit order would state a price below the current price. A buy stop order states a price above the current price. A sell limit order would require a price above the current price. A sell stop order includes a price below the current price.

In an earlier example, a client sold short 100 shares of GE at 70. Should the price rise above 70, he will lose money on the position. He is aware that this loss is potentially unlimited and wishes to reduce his exposure. Perhaps he is willing to risk a loss of about 5 points. He enters the following order:

Buy   100   GE   75   Stop

When GE is trading at $70 a share, it is quite easy to purchase at 75. But this is not what the buy stop order indicates. The client wishes to buy only if the stock rises in value to $75. His true desire is for the stock to go down to 60, 50, or 40 so that he can profit on his short sale. The stop order is simply a form of protection if he is wrong in his market strategy. Suppose GE stock does go up. It rises to 72, 73, then 74. Later the rally continues, and the shares hit 74½ and 75. When the price reaches 75, his stock order is elected, which means that the order is now transformed into a market order and the shares are purchased at the best available price. The price may be slightly more or less than 75 — perhaps 75¼ — because the elected order is now executed at the best price available.

As a result, the short has been covered. Although the client experienced a loss of 5 points or so, the possibility of unlimited loss had been eliminated. When stop orders are entered on the Exchange, they are generally entrusted to a specialist. In order to maintain an orderly market in a security, the specialist is always present at the trading post at which the stock trades. He will be in a position to execute the order once the stop price has been reached.

Stop orders can also be used to protect profits in short positions. Suppose that shortly after the short sale at $70, GE declined to $55 a share. On paper, the client has a 15-point profit. He believes that GE will drop still further and is not yet ready to cover the short, but neither does he wish to risk the loss of his profit. The following order could solve his problem:

Buy   100   GE   60   Stop

If the price decline in GE continues, his profit on the short position will increase. But if GE rises to 60, his stop order will be elected and he will purchase 100 shares at about that price. He retains approximately 10 points of profit against his short sale at $70. Had he not placed the stop order, the entire profit may have eroded and may even have turned into a loss.

One problem with stop orders is that the price at which the order will be executed is not certain. For example, with the customer's buy stop order at 60 in place, GE rises to that level. The specialist is now instructed to buy 100 shares at the market. Suppose the best price then available is $63 a share. The stock will be purchased at that price and the short covered. The stop price of 60 was not a limit placed on the order but only the level that, when reached, transformed the order into a market order. While a jump in price from 60 to 63 is most unlikely in stocks such as GE, this potential problem can be eliminated by using a form, or order, called a *stop limit order*.

With GE trading at 55, the client enters the following order:

Buy   100   GE   60   Stop   Limit   61

In this case, if GE hits 60 the stop order does not become a market order, but a limit order at $61 a share. The client is willing to pay 61 but no more. Naturally, he will be pleased to pay less than 61 if that is possible, but 61 is his limit. The problem with a stop limit order is that it may not be executed at all. If the stock trades at $60 and immediately jumps up to 63, the stop limit order to buy at 61 will not be filled; the customer has not covered his short. His profit is declining, and a loss in his position is looming on the horizon. Stop orders provide a degree of protection, but they are not a perfect solution to the risk of short selling. Look at another method of reducing the short seller's risk.

EQUITY OPTIONS

Options on equity securities have been available in the marketplace for decades, but they became a more meaningful factor when they were admitted to trading on exchanges in 1973. Equity options have many applications in the world of investing, but of particular interest is the role they may play in short selling. First, a brief description of equity options is in order.

Equity options are contracts that give the holder of the option the right to buy or sell a particular number of shares of an agreed security at a predetermined price for a period of time. These options are divided into two types—*puts* and *calls*. A put gives the holder the right to sell. A call gives the holder the right to buy.

Suppose you purchased the following option:

| 1 | Loews | Aug | 115 | Put | Premium | 5 |

Analyze the items in this contract:

1	The number of contracts. Each contract generally represents 100 shares of the underlying stock.
Loews	The name of the company whose stock is the subject of the option. Usually referred to as the underlying stock.
Aug	The expiration month, in this example, August. Options expire at 11:59 P.M. eastern standard time on the Saturday following the third Friday of the stated month.
115	The price at which the contract will be settled, $115 a share. This is referred to as the *exercise* price or *strike* price.
Put	The type of option, put or call.
Premium 5	The amount the buyer of the option pays to the seller. Since the premium is measured in dollars per share, the amount represented here is $500 ($5 × 100 shares).

As the owner of this option, you have the right to sell (put) 100 shares of Loews stock at $115 a share at any time between the date you purchased the put and its expiration in August. You can exercise this privilege even if Loews stock declines to $105 a share during that period.

Here is the whole picture. If you have the right to sell, then another party has the obligation to buy. This party is the writer, or the person who provided you with the option. Thus, you bought and someone else sold (wrote) this contract. But the writer has assumed a great deal of risk. If Loews stock declines to $50 a share before the put expires, the writer is still obligated to buy at $115. For assuming this risk, you, the buyer, pay him a fee, or premium. Perhaps the premium is 5. The premium is measured in terms of dollars per share in the contract. As in almost all cases, an equity option represents 100 shares of stock and you pay the writer $500. This is your cost for receiving the privilege to sell the stock. The premium is also the fee received by the writer for agreeing to assume the risk involved under the terms of the contract.

The writer of an options contract is in effect a short seller. He has created the option. Options are not issued by the companies whose underlying stock they represent; they are given life by the person who writes them. At a given point in time, the options outstanding on the stock of a particular company could represent more than the total number of shares outstanding.

When an option is created, the writer is said to be either covered or uncovered. A covered writer has some other position that will enable him to complete the contract. For example, if a person wrote "1 Syntex Sep 60 Call," she could be covered in a number of different ways:

1. She may own Syntex common stock. If the call is exercised against her, she has the stock to deliver.
2. She owns an exchangeable security, such as a convertible bond. If the call is exercised, she can exchange the bonds for Syntex stock and make delivery.
3. She owns (is long) a Syntex call. If the call that she wrote is exercised against her, she would exercise her own call enabling her to make delivery.

The writer of a put can also be covered. A client writes "1 Pfizer Aug 65 Put." This contract requires him to purchase 100 shares of Pfizer stock if the put is exercised against him. If he deposits the necessary funds, $6,500, in his account, he will be covered. He will also be covered if he owns (is long) a put on Pfizer. If he is required to buy the stock (is put), he exercises the put that he owns and sells the shares.

The trading of options was greatly simplified with the creation of the Options Clearing Corporation (OCC). The OCC issues all options, receives payment of premiums, and maintains the records regarding the long and short positions of firms dealing in options.

Unlike most other securities, there are no certificates used in the trading of listed options.

The identity of the buyers and writers is kept by the OCC. If you buy a call through your broker, perhaps Merrill Lynch, the transaction is recorded on the OCC records. Merrill Lynch's position in this particular option is increased by one. You own the call, but you will not receive a certificate.

When a client wishes to exercise an option, a notice is sent to the OCC, which then assigns this exercise against some firm whose client has written this same option. These assignments are made at random. The call may have originally been purchased from a client of Goldman Sachs, but when the exercise notice is assigned, it may be to Kidder Peabody & Co., which also has a client who had written this option.

The use of the OCC makes options trading more convenient than trading in stocks or bonds. It also allows the firms that deal in these contracts to save a great deal of money in their operating costs.

Suppose you bought the following option:

1   Exxon   Jan   45   Call   -   Premium   3 1/2

Under the terms of this contract, you have the right to purchase (call) 100 shares of Exxon at $45 a share until expiration next January. The writer has agreed to sell shares at that price. If Exxon goes up to $65 a share, the writer must provide you with stock at $45. For assuming this risk, you pay him a premium of $350 (100 shares × 3½).

The premiums on options transactions are negotiated between the parties to the trade. The factors that determine the premiums are the intrinsic value of the option, the volatility of the stock, and the length of time until expiration.

For example, if Exxon had been trading at $46 a share when the above option was created, the call would have been intrinsically worth 1 point. The option allows the holder to buy at 45; the stock is at 46. The intrinsic value is usually referred to as being *in the money*.

Suppose this option was written in October. As it does not expire until January, the contract still has three months to live. The premium should be greater than an option expiring in December with only two months remaining. Although time cannot be measured in dollars, it is a factor in determining the premium.

In addition, some stocks have a very high degree of volatility; they experience wide price movements. This increases the premium value of options on these securities since the buyer's opportunity to profit is increased, as is the risk taken by the writer.

To illustrate the variations in options premiums, note the two following examples. These are actual options prices that existed on the same trading day.

Hitachi	Oct	105	Call	-	Premium	8 3/8
	Market Price		104 3/4			
Chemical Bank	Sep	25	Call	-	Premium	2 3/4
	Market Price		27			

The Hitachi call is *out of the money*. It gives the holder the right to purchase stock at $105 a share, yet the stock is only trading at $104¾ a share. The buyer is willing to pay 8⅜ points premium to purchase the call. For him to break even at expiration in October, Hitachi stock would have to be worth $113⅜ a share. He would have to pay 105 to exercise the call, and he has already expended 8⅜ points in premium. This break-even figure of 113⅜ does not even consider the expenses involved in the transaction. Why did the buyer pay this price?

While this call has no intrinsic value, it does have two other valuable characteristics. At the time this transaction took place, the call had approximately five months until expiration. That is a long time in stock market terms. Hitachi stock could experience a major increase in value during that period. Hitachi shares can be somewhat volatile. In the fifty-two weeks preceding this transaction, the shares had ranged from a low price of approximately $92 to a high price of above $117. Options premiums tend to reflect volatility.

On the other hand, look at the Chemical Bank call. With an exercise price of 25, the option is 2 points in the money, as the current market value is 27. The holder of the call could buy at 25 and sell at 27. Yet the premium is only 2¾ points, just ¾ point more than the intrinsic value. This option has four months until expiration, and the shares have not shown a high volatility factor. While these factors cannot be measured precisely, the market does recognize their existence—hence, the disparity in premiums.

Equity Call Options

Puts and calls can be an important tool in protecting short positions. Either type can be used effectively. First look at the application of equity call options.

In the earlier example cited, the client sold GE stock short at 70 a share. He can protect this position at a minimal cost by using call options. He might enter the following order:

Buy   1   GE   Sep   70   Call   -   Premium 2 1/2

Through the purchase of this option, the client limits his loss on the short position to 2½ points (plus any transaction costs). Suppose GE rises in price to $90 a share. The client will exercise the call and purchase stock at 70 to cover the short. Since the short sale was made at 70, there is no profit or loss resulting. However, the client does pay $250 (2½-point premium) for the call. He loses this amount, but it becomes almost insignificant when measured against the 20-point loss he would have if he had not purchased the call. The call provided protection for the short position. Look at it as an insurance policy. With insurance you also pay a premium for protection; you hope that you will never need the benefits, but it is quite risky to be without it.

The client's maximum loss is 2½ points. What is his maximum potential profit?

While it is certainly unlikely, GE stock could become worthless. If that were to occur, the client could acquire shares at no cost to cover the short sale made at 70. His profit would be $6,750. This consists of the $7,000 in proceeds from the short sale less the $250 premium paid to purchase the call. No one expects GE stock to become worthless, but examine the maximum possibility. The lowest possible score attainable in a round of golf is 18. This requires the player to have a hole in one on each hole. This is possible, but highly improbable for even the most talented professional. Our short seller would be very pleased to cover the short sale at $60 a share. This would give him a profit of $750: the $1,000 gain from the short sale at 70 less the $250 paid in option premiums.

Equity Put Options

A short position can also be protected by utilizing put options rather than call options. In this case, the potential loss cannot be measured exactly, but a degree of protection will be provided. Look at an example of the short sale technique applied to accommodate other transactions.

A large brokerage firm has an order from a client to purchase 300,000 shares of Pepsi Co. Inc. at $70 a share. Try as it may, the brokerage firm can find only 250,000 shares for sale at that price. Rather than lose the entire order and the generous commission it will earn, the firm itself sells the remaining 50,000 shares short to the client. The transaction is completed and the commission goes to the firm, but it must now be concerned with the short position. It can, as explained earlier, purchase calls on the 50,000 shares and thus limit its possible loss. But this would cost money, as the firm would be required to pay out the necessary premiums. It elects instead to move in a different direction and sell (write) puts on Pepsi Co. Inc. stock. This does not eliminate the risk, but it does provide some protection. Brokerage firms who trade in securities for their own account are accustomed to risk. It is an integral part of their business.

The following order is entered:

Sell (Write) 500 Pepsi Co Inc Oct 70 Puts - Premium 3

Since each put option represents 100 shares of stock, the 500 puts represent 50,000 shares. The broker receives the premium of $3 per share, or a total of $150,000. If Pepsi Co. stock declines to $65 a share, the holders of the puts will exercise their options and the firm will be required to purchase 50,000 shares at $70 a share. But this would be a favorable result. By purchasing the stock at 70, the firm would cover the short sale made at the same price. There is no profit or loss. In addition to any commissions made on the original trade, the firm could also keep the $150,000 in premiums received. It will have had a very successful experience.

Suppose instead that Pepsi Co. stock goes up, and the brokerage firm is required to cover the short sale made at 70. By writing the put options, it received $3 a share in premiums and can cover as high as $73 with no loss. If the firm purchases stock below 73, it will retain some portion of the 3-point premium received. There is, however, a risk: if Pepsi Co. rises above 73, the short will be covered at a loss. The amount of loss is not measurable, but some protection was provided by writing the puts. If this had not been done, the loss would have begun to accumulate as soon as the stock rose above $70 a share. In this example, no loss appears until the stock rises higher than $73 a share. Remember that the members of the brokerage firm are market professionals who should know their business. Barring unforeseen events, such as a merger or sensational announcement of positive news by the company, the 3 points should provide adequate protection.

OPTIONS AS A SUBSTITUTE FOR SELLING SHORT

To this point, the discussion has focused on the use of equity options to protect short positions. But the versatility of options also allows you to use them as a market technique in lieu of a short position. When a short seller expects a market decline, she profits if her prediction turns out to be correct. Perhaps she feels that MMM stock trading at $85 a share is due for a drop in value. She might enter the following order:

Sell	100	MMM	Market	Short

The order would be executed on the New York Stock Exchange at 85, and the short position established. This action has a number of drawbacks. First, under the margin account requirements discussed in Chapter Six, the client would have to deposit 50 percent of the proceeds of the sale into her account; a short sale of 100 shares at 85 would call for a margin of $4,250. This is a substantial sum that might even increase if MMM stock goes higher in price. She would also be debited for any dividends paid on these shares while she remained short; these payments would be transferred to the party who loaned her the stock to facilitate the short sale. In addition, she would face the possibility of unlimited loss if her short side was wrong. It is true that she would profit if MMM stock declined in value, but she can attain virtually the same result at less cost and with far less risk by employing equity options. She can approach this goal in one of two ways: put options or call options.

First look at put options as a substitute for selling short. The client enters the following order:

Buy 1 MMM Oct 85 Put - Premium 3

The total cost for this position is the premium of $300, which also represents her entire risk. If MMM stock goes up to $90, $100, or even $200 a share, she loses only $300. She simply allows the option to expire in October and takes the loss. Obviously, she will not sell (put) the stock at 85 if its market value is higher, so she assumes a modest loss and moves on to her next undertaking. But her potential for profit in this position is almost as large as that associated with a short sale of the stock. Again, based on possibilities rather than probabilities, her potential profit on the short sale is $8,500, but on the purchase of the put this potential drops to $8,200. In the unlikely case that MMM stock becomes worthless, the client can acquire the stock at no cost. If she had sold short, she would now deliver the shares to the original lender, and the entire proceeds of the short sale at 85 ($8,500) would be hers. Since she has purchased the put option, however, she can now exercise her option, and the writer of the put is required to pay the strike price of 85. She receives $8,500 less her premium of $300 for a profit of $8,200. Since she risked only a small amount of money, perhaps the option position was worth the difference in her gain.

To use a more practical example, suppose MMM declines to $75 a share. If the client had sold short at 85, she could cover at the lower price and make $1,000. If she had elected to purchase the put, she could now purchase stock at 75, exercise the option, and be paid 85. She would have made a profit of $1,000 and, considering her premium cost, a net gain of $700.

In the preceding example the client was selling short, but her approach could as easily be applied to long positions. Why buy IBM stock at $120 a share? This would require a $6,000 margin account deposit (50 percent). The client would have to borrow the remaining $6,000 from her broker and pay interest on the loan. She would also have to assume a risk of $12,000 in the event that IBM stock became worthless. Instead, why not purchase as follows:

| 1 | IBM | Oct | 120 | Call | - | Premium | 4 1/2 |

With this purchase, her total investment and amount at risk are equal to the $450 paid in premiums. If the stock goes down, that will be the client's loss. If the stock goes higher in value, her profit will be the same as in a long position, less the $450 premium. If IBM goes up to $140 a share, the purchaser of the stock at 120 will be ahead by $2,000. The buyer of the 120 call can exercise the option, sell the stock at 140, and acquire a net gain of $1,550 ($2,000 profit − $450 premium).

At first glance the strategy of using options seems so attractive that one might ask the question, Why buy stocks or sell them short? Options seem to be a far more sensible approach. There must be a negative factor in this strategy; it looks too easy. Of course, there is. Simply stated: options expire, stocks do not.

The client who purchased the MMM Oct 85 Put must not only be correct in her market judgment, but must be correct by a fixed date. If MMM stock declines to $70 a share in November, it is too late to benefit the client, whose put expired in October. The short seller, however, may still short the stock and profit from the position in December, January, or later. The most astute market professional must admit that it is extremely difficult to predict short-term market movements. To be asked to predict them correctly by a specific date makes the problem far more complex.

Time is also the enemy of the client who bought the IBM call instead of buying the underlying shares. She is faced with an October expiration. A major upward price movement for IBM in November or December will not profit her. Her option by then is just a memory.

Call options can also be used as a substitute for short selling. In the earlier example the client who believed that MMM stock would decline purchased a put on the stock rather than sell the shares short. She could have chosen to purchase a call instead and enter the following order:

Sell (Write) 1 MMM Oct 85 Call - Premium 4

The client would have received the premium of $400. If the stock had declined to a price below 85, the call would not have been exercised. The buyer of the option will not pay her 85 if the shares are actually trading below 85. So the option writer retains the $400 profit. She has, however, undertaken a great risk. If MMM stock is above $85 a share at the expiration date, the call will be exercised and she will be required to deliver stock at the strike price. If she has no other access to the stock, she will be required to purchase the shares in the open market. The only protection she has is the $400 premium she receives for writing the call. If she can purchase shares below $89 a share (strike price 85 plus 4-point premium), she will retain some of the premium received. If she has purchased the stock at $89 a share, she will break even. Any price above $89 represents a loss, the potential for which cannot be measured. Writing calls in lieu of selling short is an alternative. Generally the call will have a higher break-even point but a shorter time within which to make a profit.

STRADDLES AND COMBINATIONS

Equity options and short sales of stock are often combined to produce imaginative market strategies. One such approach involves an option position called a *straddle*. A straddle consists of a put and a call on the same stock, with the same strike price and the same

expiration month. The position can be established as a long straddle, in which the client purchases the put and call, or as a short
straddle, in which the client sells (writes) each option.

Straddles are used to profit from the degree of volatility that the
underlying stock will experience during the life of the options. If
a wide price fluctuation is expected, a long straddle is employed.
If a very narrow price movement is anticipated, a short straddle
may prove successful.

As an example of a long straddle, assume that Atlantic Richfield
stock is trading at $115 a share. An options trader is convinced that
the price of this stock will change substantially over the coming
months, but he is not sure in which direction—up or down—this
change will occur. So he creates a long straddle by executing the
following order:

Buy 1 Atlantic Richfield Jun 115 Put - Premium 3

Buy 1 Atlantic Richfield Jun 115 Call - Premium 4

Note that all of the elements in these options—the underlying
stock, the strike price, and the expiration month—are the same.
The premiums are different, but that is a factor of the market conditions existing at this time. The position is created in mid-April
of the year, so the options have about two months before expiring
in June. The trader has invested a total of 7 points, or $700, in
premium costs. The put price is 3 ($300) and the call premium is
4 ($400). In order for the trader to turn a profit *at expiration* in June,
Atlantic Richfield stock must be more than 7 points higher or lower
than the 115 strike price. Naturally, this can occur prior to the expiration date, but when the expiration date arrives in June, the options will have no remaining time value. Only the intrinsic value
will exist. If the stock is up or down exactly 7 points at expiration,
the client will break even (excluding expenses). If Atlantic Richfield is $122 a share in June, the trader can exercise his call at 115
and sell the shares. The $700 profit will offset his total premium
cost. Any price above 115 will represent a profit that technically
is unlimited.

The client will also break even if Atlantic Richfield is trading at $108 a share at expiration. He can purchase stock at that price, exercise his 115 put, and show a $700 profit that refunds his premium expenses. Any price below 108 will bring him a profit, and if Atlantic Richfield goes out of business, his put can earn 108 points. In any case, his maximum loss will be $700. If Atlantic Richfield is selling at $115 a share at expiration, neither the put nor the call will have any value. They will both expire, and he will be out the $700 premium cost. This is highly unlikely but possible. If the stock is at 117 at expiration, his 115 call will be worth $200, cutting his loss from $700 to $500.

Traders have different opinions about the direction of the market. If that were not so, there would not be a market. If everyone thinks that a stock is going up, who will sell? Likewise, a unanimous opinion that a stock is going down will cause buyers to evaporate. Markets are built upon a diversity of opinions.

For example, another options trader concludes that Atlantic Richfield stock will experience very minor price movement in the upcoming months. She puts her opinion to the test by creating a short straddle with the following orders:

Sell
(Write) 1 Atlantic Richfield Jun 115 Put - Premium 3
Sell
(Write) 1 Atlantic Richfield Jun 115 Call - Premium 4

In this case the options trader is selling the two options short. She receives the $700 in premiums. Her contention is that Atlantic Richfield stock will not rise 7 points above or fall 7 points below the strike, or exercise, price when the options expire in June. If she is correct, she will retain some but probably not all of the premiums received.

In June, if the stock is trading at $112 a share, the 115 put the options trader wrote will be exercised against her, and she will be required to buy 100 shares of Atlantic Richfield at that price. If she sells it immediately, she will sustain a $300 loss, leaving her with a $400 overall profit from her short sales.

We must also look at the risk that this options trader has assumed. If the options are written with no offsetting position to protect her, she has a loss potential that cannot be measured. She has written a call with a strike price of 115. If the stock is above that price at expiration, it will be exercised against her, and she will have to deliver 100 shares at $115 a share. If she has no stock, she will have to buy it. At what price? That question cannot be answered. Atlantic Richfield might be at 120, 130, 150, or 200—select any number you wish. In any case, a loss will result. If the loss exceeds the $700 the options trader received when she wrote the options, she will be a net loser.

The same problem exists with the put. Suppose that at expiration the stock is selling at $100 a share, and the options trader is put at 115. An immediate sale of the stock at its current price results in a $1,500 loss. When the premium is deducted, her net loss is $800.

In our prior example of a long straddle, the trader could lose no more than the amount paid for the premium ($700) although that is unlikely: as the stock goes up, the call goes into the money; and as the stock goes down, the put goes into the money. The loss in writing a short straddle, however, cannot be measured. This is not unusual. In nearly every case, a short position contains more risk than a long position.

The trader who wrote the short straddle does not have to wait until June to take action. If Atlantic Richfield stock declines to 113 in May, she might cover her short put by buying 1 June 115 Put at a premium of 5. When measured against her original sale price of 3, she sustains a $200 loss. But she still has the $400 premium from the sale of the call, and perhaps, if the stock continues to decline, she will retain that and show an overall profit of $200.

Traders must be agile. Unlike investors, who take a position and stay with it for long period of time, traders must move very quickly, as opportunities appear or necessity dictates. The investor is the tortoise; the trader the hare. But the outcome is not always the same as in the old fable.

A straddle consists of a put and a call on the same security, each option having the same strike price and the same expiration month.

In a similar strategy, an investor could use options in which either the strike price and/or the expiration month is different. For example:

Buy
   1 Atlantic Richfield Jun 115 Put - Premium 3

Buy
   1 Atlantic Richfield Jun 120 Call - Premium 2

While the security and the expiration month are the same for each option, the strike prices are different. When such a difference is present the strategy is called a combination.

Although short selling of stocks and short selling of options as market tools can produce profits or protect positions, some strategies utilize short sales of both products in quest of gains.

One such strategy is based on the premise that professional options traders often write options with the goal of retaining the premium received. In the short straddle, the trader wrote two options, a put and a call, on the same stock. Her goal was to keep all or part of the $700 paid to her in premiums. But such a strategy entails a large risk.

Another strategy combines a short straddle with a long position in the underlying stock. The goal again is to earn money from the premiums paid. This strategy is used only if the trader feels that the price of the underlying stock is going higher. It is a bullish strategy.

This may at first seem to contradict earlier statements. You have seen that short sales are generally employed when the trader foresees a declining market. This strategy would appear to be opposed to that theory, but it is not. Generally, short sales are made to profit from a decline in value of the stock, which allows the short sale to be covered at a favorable price. In this case, however, the aim is to retain options premiums. Look at an example of this trading device:

Long stock
Short straddle

A trader feels that IBM stock will rise in price from its current level of $120 a share. He could, of course, purchase the stock, but he would lose money if he were wrong and the stock declined below 120. Instead, he executes the following orders:

Buy   100   IBM   120

Sell (Write)   1 IBM Oct 120 Put - Premium 5

Sell (Write)   1 IBM Oct 120 Call - Premium 6

He is now long 100 shares of IBM stock, and short 1 IBM put and 1 IBM call. He has taken in $1,100 in premiums ($500 for the put and $600 for the call).

The trader proves correct in his market judgment, and IBM rises to $130 a share. The 120 call that he wrote will surely be exercised, but this causes no problem. He owns the stock and delivers it in accordance with the contract terms. Since his cost of the stock is also 120, he has no profit or loss. He is now left with 1 IBM Oct 120 *short* Put, but that option will certainly not be exercised. Why would the holder of the put sell stock at $120 a share when the market price is $130? As a result, the trader retains the $1,100 in premiums received for writing the options.

Of course, there is risk; there always is. If IBM had declined instead of rising in value, the 120 put would be exercised against him. He would now own 200 shares of IBM: the 100 shares purchased at $120 when he implemented his strategy and the 100 shares he purchased at $120 when the put was exercised. All of these shares were purchased at $120 a share. Suppose IBM stock was trading at $115 a share. Would our trader have a profit or loss? He would in fact, have a profit of $100. If he sold 200 shares at 115, he would incur a 5-point loss per share, as each share cost him 120, and total loss would be $1,000.

But the trader collected $1,100 in premiums, and he is still $100 ahead. The protection provided by the premiums is not limitless. If he loses more than $1,100 on the sale of the stock, he has a net loss. But the risk may be worth it. It is his decision.

This position can be altered if the trader is bearish on IBM. In this case, he would execute these orders:

| Sell | | 100 | IBM | 120 | Short |

| Sell | (Write) | 1 | IBM | Oct | 120 | Put | - | Premium | 5 |

| Sell | (Write) | 1 | IBM | Oct | 120 | Call | - | Premium | 6 |

If IBM declines to $110 a share, the put is exercised against him. The shares thus purchased will be used to cover the short sale made at the same price (120), thereby resulting in no profit or loss. He is now short a worthless call with a strike price of 120 and has $1,100 in premiums in his pocket.

If IBM rises, contrary to his prediction, he will be called and will now be short 200 shares. But he does have $1,100 to protect him from loss when he covers the short positions. This works out to 5½ points per share ($1,100 divided by 200), so he would not lose money if he covers the short at 125½ or lower.

OPTIONS ON OTHER PRODUCTS

To this point, our discussion has been limited to options or stocks of corporations. These are called equity options. But options are also traded on other financial instruments. These options, which are also very actively employed by short sellers, are worthy of attention.

There are three major categories: (1) index options, (2) foreign currency options, and (3) interest rate options. These options are very similar to equity options and have many of the same characteristics. Each has two types, puts and calls, and each has a specific strike price and expiration month. As with equity options, the premium is determined by negotiation between the buyer and the seller. The differences are found in the underlying product and, in some cases, the manner in which settlement occurs. The basic applications are the same. They are used to participate in upward or downward market movements or to protect other positions. But because the underlying product is different, the reasons for their use differ as well.

Index Options

While an equity option records the movement of one particular stock, perhaps GE, an index option traces the movement of a large group of stocks. The use of indexes to measure overall market performance has been a factor in market analysis for more than a century. The Dow Jones Average, the most often cited measurement, can be traced back to 1885. Among the many other indexes currently in use are those compiled by Standard & Poors Corp., the New York Stock Exchange, and Value Line Inc. While these statistics were valuable to investors, they were not products that could be bought or sold. The introduction of index options changed that situation. It is now possible to buy and sell options based on a particular stock index. This enables an investor to participate in general market movements, rather than being restricted to the price changes in only one stock. If, for example, you thought that CBS stock was going down, you might purchase a put on that stock, which will have much the same result as selling the stock short. Subsequent to your purchase of the CBS put, the stock market suffers a severe decline. All stocks drop sharply in value, except CBS. That stock resists the trend and remains steady or may even rise in price. The market went down. You had bought a put. You should be a winner, but you are not. Index options permit a client to be less specific in his selection. Your study of market indicators leads you to believe that a decline is in the offing. You may purchase an index option put.

The most popular index option is based on the Standard & Poors 100 stock index. A value is set each trading date. When originally introduced, the value was 100, considering the value of the component stocks on that date. As those prices have varied, so has the value of the index. Figure 7.1 indicates that, on the day in question, the value of the S&P 100 index was 366.77. (Note: The S&P 100 index is usually referred to as the OEX, which is the symbol used to identify it on the automated stock ticker.)

Friday, May 25, 1990

Options closing prices. Sales unit usually is 100 shares.
Stock close is New York or American exchange final price.

MOST ACTIVE OPTIONS

CHICAGO BOARD

	Sales	Last	Chg.	N.Y. Close
CALLS				
SP100 Jun340	22419	3½	– 2¾	336.77
SP100 Jun345	15369	1⅞	– 1⅞	336.77
SP100 Jun335	12984	6¼	– 3⅜	336.77
SP100 Jun350	7706	15-16	–1 1-16	336.77
I B M Jun120	4967	13-16	–11-16	116⅜
PUTS				
SP100 Jun340	22946	6⅜	+ 1¾	336.77
SP100 Jun335	17888	3⅞	+15-16	336.77
SP100 Jun330	9794	2⅝	+ ⅝	336.77
SP100 Jun325	8860	1¾	+ ⅜	336.77
SP100 Jun320	4480	1 5-16	+ 5-16	336.77

AMERICAN

	Sales	Last	Chg.	N.Y. Close
CALLS				
Ph Mor Jun45	4853	¼	– ⅜	42⅝
Ph Mor Jun40	2295	3	– 1½	42⅝
Ph Mor Jul45	1945	¾	– ⅝	42⅝
Apple Jun40	1588	1 5-16	–1 5-16	40
Dig Eq Jun95	1419	1⅛	– 3-16	92½
PUTS				
Apple Jun40	2103	1 3-16	+ 9-16	40
Dig Eq Jun90	1664	1¼	....	92½
MMIdx Jun565	1505	6⅝	+ 1⅛	566.21
Ph Mor Jun40	1127	3-16	+ 1-16	42⅝
Lotus Jun35	1036	15-16	+ 1-16	36¼

PHILADELPHIA

	Sales	Last	Chg.	N.Y. Close
CALLS				
Avery Jul25	5092	1 11-16	–1 9-16	26¼
Bard Oct17½	2278	1	– ⅜	16⅛
GaGulf Jul7½	1215	1¾	+ 5-16	8¾
F N M Jun40	706	1 3-16	– ¼	39¾
Time Jun110	547	1⅝	– ⅞	105⅝

	Sales	Last	Chg.	N.Y. Close
PUTS				
Avery Jul25	470	⅝	– ¾	26¼
McGHII Nov50	360	1¼	....	55⅛
KayJwl Aug7½	327	1½	+ ⅛	7½
HomeD Aug55	228	2¼	+ 5-16	57⅞
BkBost Jun12½	168	5-16	+ 1-16	13⅛

PACIFIC

	Sales	Last	Chg.	N.Y. Close
CALLS				
AdobeS Jul35	2118	3¾	– 10¾	35¼
AdobeS Jun35	2108	2⅜	– 8⅛	35¼
AdobeS Jun40	1893	13-16	–9 3-16	35¼
Hilton Jun50	1257	1⅝	– ¾	50⅛
AdobeS Jul40	1226	1⅞	– 9⅛	35¼
PUTS				
AdobeS Jul30	1098	1 3-16	+ 1	35¼
TCBY Jun30	900	10⅝	+ 1⅛	19½
Micrsft Jun70	844	1¾	+ ½	74¼
SmkBEq Jun40	812	¾	+ 7-16	41
Nike Oct60	775	⅝	– 3-16	80

NEW YORK

	Sales	Last	Chg.	N.Y. Close
CALLS				
Maytag Jul17½	1107	5-16	....	16⅜
CSoup Jun55	613	⅞	– ⅜	53⅜
DigCom Jun25	398	1	– ½	25¼
DigCom Jul25	222	1⅝	– ⅝	25¼
Q M S Jun17½	217	13-16	– 1-16	17½
PUTS				
Maytag Jul17½	1002	1⅛	– ⅛	16⅜
FruitL Jul15	300	1⅝	+ ⅛	13¾
ConFrt Jun17½	176	¾	+ ⅛	17⅛
DigCom Jun25	176	13-16	+ 3-16	25¼
ConFrt Jul15	175	½	....	17⅛

Figure 7.1. Typical listing of most active options from the financial page of a daily newspaper.

Interestingly, on this day, the S&P 100 was the most active option traded on the Chicago Board, for both puts and calls. In fact, it accounted for nine of the ten most active options to trade that day.

The trading of index options does not vary from that of equity options. A trader is very bearish on the market in general. He cannot sell short every stock on the exchange, but he can implement his feeling using index options. Since he believes that the market will decline, he has two choices, just as with equity options. He can purchase puts or he can sell (write) calls. Using the most active option in each type from the previous illustration, the trader may do the following:

Buy 1 S&P Jun 340 Put - Premium 6 3/8

The premium on an index option is determined by multiplying the price times 100. The premium for this purchase was $637.50 (100 × 6.37½).

The trader now has the right to exercise his put at a strike price of 340 until expiration in June. This option has an intrinsic value of 3.23 ($323), computed by comparing the strike price against the current index value of 336.77 ($34,000 − $33,677). The market, and this index, declines still further, and at expiration in June, the S&P 100 index stands at 329.80. The put with the 340 strike price has an in-the-money value of $1,020. The strike price of 340.00 minus the current value of 329.80 equals 10.20. By applying the multiplier of 100 ($10.20 × 100), the trader arrives at $1,020; he decides to exercise his option. But unlike equity options, he does not deliver stock. It would be rather impractical to deliver 100 stocks separately as a form of exercise. No, index options are settled in cash. The trader sends an exercise notice to the OCC, and his account will be credited with $1,020 in cash. If he had been wrong, he would have allowed his option to expire. His loss would have been limited to the $637.50 paid in premiums.

Instead of buying the put, he could have written a call:

Sell (Write) 1 S&P 100 Jun 340 Call - Premium 3 1/2

Had the market declined to 329.80 at expiration, the call would not have been exercised against him and he would have kept the $350 in premiums. A trader cannot sell the entire market short, but index options provide an alternative method of accomplishing this goal.

Index options can also be used to protect long or short positions. Suppose a firm that actively traded in the market had established a large number of short positions in anticipation of a market decline. If the decline did not occur, the firm would incur great losses. It might hedge the short positions using index options. It could choose to buy calls or write puts.

If it purchased an appropriate number of S&P 100 calls, a rise in the market would increase the value of these calls. This would act to offset the loss suffered in the short positions. The firm might instead write S&P 100 puts. Should the market rise, the puts would not be exercised and the premiums received would minimize its losses.

Index options can also be used to protect large investment portfolios. The manager of a $200 million pension fund sees a market decline on the horizon. She may not wish to liquidate her entire portfolio, but by purchasing index puts or writing index calls, she can protect her long portfolio position.

The use of index options is more than an alternative to a short sale. Since one cannot sell the whole market short, index options become a substitute rather than an alternative. A different product, but one with some similarities, index futures, will be covered in Chapter Ten.

Foreign Currency Options

With the end of World War II in 1945, most of the world's nations were in a state of economic chaos. Great Britain, France, and most of western Europe had seen their industrial facilities destroyed or damaged by years of armed conflict and occupation. Germany, Italy, and other defeated nations would require years to regain their autonomy, while eastern Europe, including a large part of Germany, became enclosed behind the Iron Curtain, remaining there until 1989. In Asia, Japan would begin a period of occupation that would stifle its economic development for nearly two decades.

The only major world power that had not suffered internal damage was the United States, which was quickly able to reverse its production priorities from wartime to peacetime necessities. For a long period, the United States would be the prominent supplier and donator of the goods needed by most of the world. The dollar became not only the most stable currency but, in many situations, the only currency. Virtually all international transactions were made in terms of dollars or in the dollar equivalent of the local currency.

In time, the world returned to a more diversified market as Europe and Japan made remarkable strides forward. Nations that had little impact on world trade prior to the war, such as Korea and Taiwan, moved into the international trading arena. No longer was the United States the single dominant factor in the world of economics. When television made its first impact as a consumer product in the late 1940s, it was nearly impossible to find a set that was not manufactured by an American company. By 1990, it would be just as impossible to locate one that was. But despite the growth of competition from other nations, the U.S. dollar remained the standard for international trade. With the increase in world dealings in petroleum products, the Arab nations that were the main exporters of that product formed OPEC (Organization of Petroleum Exporting Countries). Prices for the oil, however, were stated in dollars.

The value of a nation's currency was measured in U.S. dollars. Naturally, these exchange rates would fluctuate as conditions changed. You have to be fifty years old or more to remember when the term pound meant $5. If you asked your brother to lend you a pound, you were asking for $5. The reference was to the exchange rate of a British pound to a U.S. dollar. In years past, the equivalent of one British pound was $5. That rate has varied over the years and at one point nearly reached parity—1 pound equaling $1—but has more often hovered between $1.50 and $2.10 to a pound. As tourism and international trade increased, people of all nations were required to become familiar with the value of other currencies. When you traveled to Germany and considered purchasing a fine sweater for 30 marks, you needed to translate this into your own currency to see if you had found a bargain. If the German mark was worth $0.60 at the time, then 30 marks equaled $18. Traders and businesspeople began to trade in the various currencies of the world. If you thought the German mark at $0.60 would soon be worth more, you might purchase $100,000 worth of that currency.

If the mark rose to $0.65, you could exchange your holdings for $108,333 in U.S. currency.

Mark at $0.60: $100,000 ÷ $0.60 = 166,666 marks
Mark at $0.65: 166,666 marks × $0.65 = $108,333

This is not a bad profit, but quite difficult to deal in. A great deal of cash was needed, and should the currency fluctuate in the wrong direction, the losses could be substantial. To ease the problem for both traders and businesspeople, a market developed for options on foreign currencies. Both buyers and short sellers can use these contracts to their advantage. We will look at them from the viewpoint of the short seller.

The Philadelphia Stock Exchange trades options in seven foreign currencies and on European currency units (ECUs). The size of each contract varies with the country and is based on the number of units of each foreign currency represented by each contract:

Currency	Units per contract
Australian dollar	50,000
British pound	31,250
Canadian dollar	50,000
German mark	62,500
French franc	250,000
Japanese yen	6,250,000
Swiss franc	62,500
European currency units	62,500

The trading is similar to that in equity options with a number of strike prices available in each of three expiration months. Both puts and calls are listed. With the exception of the French franc and Japanese yen contracts, the premiums are quoted in cents per dollar. The French franc quote is in $0.001ths per unit, and the yen is quoted $0.0001ths per unit.

To determine the total premiums, multiply the stated value by the number of units in the particular contract. For example, a call on British pounds with a strike price of $1.675, expiring in June with a premium of 1.30 would have a total value of $406.25.

Size of Contract	×	Premium	=	Total
31,250	×	$0.0130	=	$406.25

A chart of a typical day of currency options trading on the Philadelphia Exchange is shown in Figure 7.2.

A trader is bearish on the German mark. He feels that economic growth is slowing in that nation and that their currency will decline in relation to the U.S. dollar. He could implement this theory by selling calls on that currency. In effect, he is shorting the West German mark:

Sell (Write) 1 German Mark Jul 60 At .42

The total premium received for writing this call was $262.50 (62,500 marks × $0.42 cents per unit). He has given the buyer the right to purchase marks at $0.60 each until the contract expires in July. At the time the contract was created, the mark was valued at $0.5885. Should it decline or even remain at that level, the holder of the call would surely not exercise and pay $0.60 per mark. The short seller keeps the $262.50 premium received. The usual dangers of selling short do exist. If the mark rises above $0.60 in value, the short seller may have to purchase the currency in the market. He may eliminate his position by repurchasing the call and covering his short. But the premium he will have to pay will no doubt be more than he received. In either case, a loss will occur.

The shorting of currency options can also be used to protect a participant in an international business transaction. An American bicycle manufacturer has contracted to sell a number of his vehicles to a British client. The value of the contract is $210,000 and is made at a time when the British pound is worth $1.68. Payment will be made in pounds and the American's profit is computed on the basis of the pound's being worth $1.68. Because payment will not be made for forty-five days or so, the manufacturer is at risk. Should the pound decline in value below $1.68 in that time period, his profit would be reduced and perhaps disappear. He makes some calculations.

OPTIONS
PHILADELPHIA EXCHANGE

Option & Underlying	Strike Price	Calls—Last			Puts—Last		
		Jun	Jul	Sep	Jun	Jul	Sep
50,000 Australian Dollars-cents per unit.							
ADollr	...73	r	3.95	r	r	0.10	r
76.96	...75	r	r	r	r	r	1.21
76.96	...77	0.37	r	r	0.71	r	r
76.96	...78	r	0.30	r	r	r	r
31,250 British Pounds-cents per unit.							
BPound	160	r	r	r	0.07	r	1.40
168.09	162½	r	r	r	0.07	0.66	r
168.09	.165	r	1.20	r	r	1.20	r
168.09	167½	1.30	1.85	r	0.80	2.05	r
168.09	.170	0.32	1.00	1.90	2.10	r	r
168.09	172½	r	0.50	r	r	r	r
31,250 British Pounds-European Style.							
168.09	167½	r	1.97	r	r	r	r
168.09	172½	r	0.50	r	r	r	r
50,000 Canadian Dollars-cents per unit.							
CDollr	.81½	r	r	r	r	r	0.31
85.20	...82	r	r	r	r	r	0.38
85.20	...83	r	r	r	0.05	r	0.63
85.20	.83½	r	r	r	0.07	r	0.80
85.20	...84	r	r	r	0.12	0.51	1.13
85.20	.84½	r	r	r	0.25	0.60	1.32
85.20	...85	0.42	0.61	0.77	r	0.85	1.75
85.20	.85½	0.20	r	r	0.82	r	2.10
85.20	...86	0.13	r	r	r	r	2.50
50,000 Canadian Dollars-European Style.							
CDollar	82½	r	r	r	r	0.15	r
85.20	.83½	r	r	1.27	r	r	r
85.20	...84	r	r	0.99	r	r	r
62,500 West German Marks-cents per unit.							
DMark	.. 57	r	r	r	r	0.23	r
58.85	...58	r	1.30	1.76	0.19	r	0.92
58.85	.58½	r	1.05	s	0.32	0.61	s
58.85	...59	0.40	0.73	r	0.56	0.76	r
58.85	.59½	0.25	r	s	r	0.85	s
58.85	...60	0.13	0.42	r	1.20	r	r
58.85	.60½	0.12	r	s	r	r	s
58.85	...61	0.06	0.21	r	r	r	2.60
58.85	.61½	r	0.17	s	r	r	s
58.85	...62	0.02	r	r	r	r	r
58.85	...63	0.02	r	0.27	r	r	3.94
58.85	...64	r	0.03	r	r	r	r
250,000 French Francs-10ths of a cent per unit.							
FFranc	.. 19	r	r	r	r	r	15.30
6,250,000 Japanese Yen-100ths of a cent per unit.							
JYen	... 62	r	r	r	r	r	0.18
65.90	...63	r	r	r	0.04	r	r
65.90	...65	1.35	r	r	0.19	r	r
65.90	.65½	r	r	s	0.23	0.52	s
65.90	...66	0.44	r	1.40	0.54	r	1.08
65.90	.66½	0.28	r	s	r	r	s
65.90	...67	0.18	r	0.97	r	r	r
65.90	.67½	0.14	r	s	r	r	s
65.90	...68	0.05	r	0.55	r	r	r
65.90	...69	r	0.15	r	r	r	r
65.90	...70	r	0.08	r	r	r	r
62,500 Swiss Francs-cents per unit.							
SFranc	.. 67	r	r	r	r	0.24	r
69.44	...68	r	r	2.65	r	0.26	0.72
69.44	.68½	r	r	s	0.21	r	s
69.44	...69	r	r	r	0.33	0.70	r
69.44	.69½	r	r	s	0.32	r	s
69.44	...70	r	0.74	r	0.89	1.20	1.83
69.44	...71	r	0.56	r	1.64	r	r
69.44	...72	r	0.36	r	r	r	r
69.44	...73	r	0.20	r	r	r	r

Total call vol. 23,367   Call open int. 368,730
Total put vol. 24,913   Put open int. 356,289
r—Not traded. s—No option offered.
Last is premium (purchase price).

Figure 7.2. Typical listing of currency option trading activity on the Philadelphia Exchange. (Copyright 1990, The Wall Street Journal. Reproduced by permission.)

With the pound at $1.68, the equivalent of $210,000 is 125,000 British pounds ($210,000 ÷ $1.68). To protect his bicycle sale, he uses the foreign currency option market and enters this order:

Sell (Write) 4 British Pound Jul 170 Calls - Premium 1.00

Since there are 31,250 pounds per contract, he has sold short calls on 125,000 pounds (31,250 × 4 contracts). He has received a premium of $0.01 per unit, which equals $1,250. If, on receipt of payment, the pound has declined to $1.67, the $0.01 premium protects his original profit computed at $1.68. Should the pound rise, he will be even more pleased. If British pounds rise to $1.72, the calls will be exercised against him. But he will be paid $1.70 per pound. Add to this the $0.01 premium received, and his contract has now been completed at $1.71 per pound. His original profit computed at $1.68 is proportionately increased.

There is, of course, risk. He is only protected down to a value of $1.67. Should the pound decline below that level, his original profit is jeopardized. The applications of foreign currency options are many and varied. The examples presented point out only the principal theories involved.

These contracts can also be used to implement transactions that do not even involve U.S. dollars. An American businessperson might import goods for later resale in Switzerland. He pays for the material in Japanese yen and receives his payment in Swiss francs. He may use option contracts on either or both of these currencies to reduce the risk of value fluctuations. The values of major world currencies are cross-referenced against each other every day. Figure 7.3 shows the relationship on a particular trading day.

Interest Rate Options

Put and call options on debt instruments are also traded in our markets. These enable traders and investors to implement their opinions on forthcoming changes in interest rates. It is an axiom of investing that if interest rates rise, the price of outstanding bonds must fall to reflect the now-current return. Conversely, should in-

Key Currency Cross Rates Late New York Trading Jun. 1, 1990

	Dollar	Pound	SFranc	Guilder	Yen	Lira	D-Mark	FFranc	CdnDlr
Canada	1.1748	1.9748	.81754	.61460	.00774	.00094	.69187	.20512	......
France	5.7275	9.628	3.9857	2.9963	.03772	.00458	3.3731	....	4.8753
Germany	1.6980	2.8543	1.1816	.88831	.01118	.00136	....	.29646	1.4454
Italy	1249.8	2100.8	869.69	653.81	8.230	....	736.01	218.20	1063.8
Japan	151.85	255.26	105.672	79.440	....	.12150	89.429	26.512	129.26
Netherlands ..	1.9115	3.2132	1.3302	....	.01259	.00153	1.1257	.33374	1.6271
Switzerland ...	1.4370	2.4156	...	.75177	.00946	.00115	.84629	.25089	1.2232
U.K.	.59488	....	.41398	.31121	.00392	.00048	.35034	.10386	.50637
U.S.	....	1.6810	.69589	.52315	.00659	.00080	.58893	.17460	.85121

Source: Telerate

Figure 7.3. Typical listing of major currency price relationships from a daily newspaper.

terest rates fall, bond prices will rise accordingly. Though interest rate options can be dealt in by anyone who wishes to do so, their use is generally limited to professional traders and institutional investors.

The AMEX and CBOE trade options on three debt instruments issued by the U.S. Treasury. Each contract on the short-term instrument, U.S. Treasury Bills, represents $1 million of face value of the underlying security and trades on the AMEX. The contracts on the longer Treasury instruments, Notes and Bonds, represent $100,000 of these securities and are traded on the CBOE.

A trader anticipating a decline in bond prices due to an increase in interest rates could write calls on these Treasury securities. Should prices in fact decline, the calls will not be exercised and the premium will be kept as a profit.

Perhaps the manager of a large pension fund is concerned about the bond market. The portfolio contains a large amount of Treasury securities, and interest rates appear to be headed higher. To sell the Treasury position would be impractical, since the income is needed to supply the required pension payments. The manager could provide some protection, as well as adding income, by writing calls against all or part of the position. The premiums earned may offset any decline in value of the portfolio due to lower bond values.

This discussion of options, which provided an overall view of their applications with a particular concern for their relationship to selling short, was of necessity quite brief. A detailed account of this important product can be found in a number of excellent books published on that subject.

8
Decision Making through Market Analysis

How does a market participant make his or her decision to sell short? More often than not such decisions are made through analysis of overall economic conditions or circumstances present in the life of a particular company. The two traditional methods of measuring a market's potential are *fundamental analysis* and *technical analysis*. The fundamental analyst studies a company's financial conditions and prospects, including the strength of the corporate balance sheet, the trend of earnings, the profit margins, and the ability of management. The technical analyst may reject this type of study and choose different criteria. As a believer in the theory that past performance is indicative of future behavior, he studies the trends of price movements and trading volume as the keys for his activity. His work may allow him to identify trends in a particular stock that, if followed, will lead to profits.

Fundamental analysis and technical analysis are much like pepper and salt. Some investors — as some eaters of scrambled eggs — use one or the other; some apply both to their market study and to their eggs. Still others prefer to employ neither.

Those who shun the traditional analytical tools often apply rather unconventional methods to dictate their market participation. A trader's very mood may be the basis of his decision. If the morning finds him bright and cheerful, with the feeling that the world could not be better, he may translate this mood into a bullish market attitude. If at the break of a different day his stomach is sour and his head is throbbing, he may roar like a bear and approach the market similarly. Does this approach work? Sometimes it does and sometimes it doesn't, but these odds can be correctly applied to any market theory. If a surefire method of making money in the market existed, no one would need to read or write books about the subject. Whatever suits you is what you should be doing. A well-respected Wall Street trader puts both horseradish and Tabasco sauce on her scrambled eggs. She is in all other ways quite a normal person. Before studying the traditional methods of market analysis, look at three unconventional market theories that have found a place in history. Their use is not being recommended here, nor is their validity being rejected. Everyone must make his or her own decisions.

THE RANDOM WALK THEORY

The rationale applied in the random walk theory is that it does not make any difference what method you use to select the stocks you buy or sell short. Use any system you like; the results will be the same. To apply this theory you might remove from the morning newspaper the tables containing the prices of all stocks. Attach these pages to a wall in your home. (Note: It is advisable to use a wall in a room not open to guests, as this theory can lead to major structural damage.) Step back thirty feet from the wall and throw with great force eight sharply pointed darts into the pages. The stock nearest the point of each dart should be sold short immediately (or, if you wish, bought). This theory does not discriminate. If you rent an apartment and are fearful that this method may lead to eviction, use another approach. Select three words often used to identify companies with publicly traded stocks—for instance, American, General, and United. On the first day, sell short the stock of the first company appearing under each designation. Day one will find you selling short American Barrick Resources, General American Investing, and United Asset Management. On day two, sell short

American Brands, General Cinema, and United Illuminating. Continue through the alphabet until you are either very rich or completely destitute. One or the other is likely to occur. The rules here allow you to change in midstream. If the Generals are not working out you can switch to Nationals.

THE HEMLINE HYPOTHESIS

This hypothesis purports that the market will move in the same direction as the hemline of women's skirts. The short seller must force himself to carefully study the legs of women he passes in the street. (Be discreet, this hypothesis does not make allowances for medical costs or attorney's fees.) If skirt lengths stop at midthigh, the time for selling short may be near. If fashion trends dictate a descending hemline, perhaps below the knee, the market is sure to fall. This theory proved to be valid in the 1960s when the miniskirt was replaced by a garment that called for more material. If skirt lengths are quite low, let the short seller beware. As the trend reverses and hemlines rise, so too will the market. The "new look" that found women wearing skirts of near-Victorian length coincided with a low point in market history. As sanity prevailed and hemlines rose, the market followed suit.

Short sellers addicted to the hemline hypothesis live by the adage, "Sell short three inches above the knee, and cover the short three inches above the ankle."

THE SUPER BOWL THEORY

Why do short sellers always root for the American Football Conference (AFC) team to defeat the National Football Conference (NFC) team in the Super Bowl each January? The reason is in no way connected with the sport. Most short sellers have enough on their minds and probably do not even follow the sport. This interest actually stems from a market theory that has proven to be amazingly accurate. It is called the Super Bowl Theory.

In June 1966, the venerable National Football League (NFL) merged with the much younger American Football League (AFL). The new entity continued to operate under the title of the National

Football League and play was conducted in two divisions – the National Football Conference (NFC) and the American Football Conference (AFC). In order to achieve numerical balance, three teams from the NFL – the Cleveland Browns, the Pittsburgh Steelers, and the Baltimore (now Indianapolis) Colts – transferred to the AFC. In January 1967, the winning teams from each conference met in a game to determine the overall football champion. In the third year of its history (1969), this game became known as the Super Bowl. In time market observers became aware of an odd circumstance: if a team originally associated with the NFL, including the three transferees, won this big game, the market as measured by the Dow Jones Industrial Average would end that year at a higher level than in the prior year; if an original AFL member became Super Bowl champion, the market would close lower for the year. If this theory has validity, then the decision of the short seller is greatly simplified. If an AFC team wins the big game, he should enter a barrage of short sale orders and wait for his fortune to be made. Since the game has always been played in January, the short seller's investment decisions for the year are made before the daffodils are in bloom. If the Super Bowl champ was originally an NFL member, the short seller should take the year off. Perhaps he can spend his time in less-dangerous pursuits like fighting oil well fires.

As of this writing, there have been 25 of these championship games. Table 8.1 identifies the winner of each game, the team's original affiliation, and the result of that year's market performance.

Through the Super Bowl of 1990, this theory has been correct in 21 of 24 years in which this game has been played. Even in the 3 years of error, the variation in the market was very minor. A slight change in each case would have resulted in a perfect score.

On Sunday, January 27, 1991, the New York Giants of the NFC defeated the Buffalo Bills of the AFC by a score of 20–19 in what may have been the most exciting Super Bowl game ever played. But this book is not about sports. Our concern is the action of the market, if this theory holds, the Giant's victory in Super Bowl XXV indicates a higher market for 1991.

Before you place your future prosperity on this unorthodox method of measuring the market, a bit more analysis is necessary.

TABLE 8.1 Super Bowl Results

Year	Champion	Original Affiliation	Dow Jones Industrial Average—Year
1967	Green Bay Packers	NFL	+ 119.42
1968	Green Bay Packers	NFL	+ 38.64
1969	NY Jets	AFL	− 143.39
1970 (A)	Kansas City Chiefs	AFL	+ 38.56
1971	Baltimore Colts	NFL	+ 51.28
1972	Dallas Cowboys	NFL	+ 129.82
1973	Miami Dolphins	AFL	− 169.16
1974	Miami Dolphins	AFL	− 234.62
1975	Pittsburgh Steelers	NFL	+ 236.17
1976	Pittsburgh Steelers	NFL	+ 152.24
1977	Oakland Raiders	AFL	− 173.48
1978 (A)	Dallas Cowboys	NFL	− 26.16
1979	Pittsburgh Steelers	NFL	+ 33.73
1980	Pittsburgh Steelers	NFL	+ 125.25
1981	Oakland Raiders	AFL	− 88.99
1982	San Francisco 49ers	NFL	+ 171.54
1983	Washington Redskins	NFL	+ 212.10
1984	LA Raiders	AFL	− 47.07
1985	San Francisco 49ers	NFL	+ 335.10
1986	Chicago Bears	NFL	+ 349.28
1987	NY Giants	NFL	+ 42.88
1988	Washington Redskins	NFL	+ 229.74
1989	San Francisco 49ers	NFL	+ 584.63
1990 (A)	San Francisco 49ers	NFL	− 119.54
1991	NY Giants	NFL	NA

(A) Theory failed

In the past 24 years, the market closed higher 17 times. In those years an original NFL team won 17 times. The market was down in 7 of the years, and an original AFL team won 7 times. No doubt the market would have gone up a majority of the years in any case. Since the NFL had the greater number of members, it would be expected that its teams would win a majority of the games. In 5 of the years—1971, 1975, 1976, 1979, and 1980—the NFL could not lose. Both teams claimed that league as its original affiliation. So this market strategy just recognizes a simple statistical fact. The market was generally higher during the time period, and the side whose winning predicted an upswing in the market had many more players. It should also be noted that short sellers generally do not plan their movements one year in advance. Most short sellers are traders and tend to close out positions relatively quickly. So enjoy the Super Bowl for what it is: an exciting sports event that fills a sometimes dreary winter Sunday afternoon.

This concludes the offbeat, unconventional theories. It is safe to say that a sufficient number of them exist with which to fill a most-interesting book. They are not, however, the standards by which most serious market participants are guided. These people prefer to be led by the more accepted methods of fundamental and technical analysis.

FUNDAMENTAL ANALYSIS

The fundamental analyst carefully studies the financial information that may affect the general economy of the country or the fortunes of a particular company. His thorough and exhausting study may lead to conclusions that indicate profitable market opportunities. While most analysts seek to uncover undervalued securities for purchase, many will arrive at decisions that lead to short sales. It is not at all uncommon for two analysts looking at the same information to come to opposite conclusions. If XYZ Corporation reports a record increase in earnings for the year, analyst A may interpret this as the beginning of a trend that will drive the price of XYZ stock higher. He recommends purchase. Analyst B, on the other hand, reads this as a one-time event not to be repeated. When her analysis is later confirmed, the inflated price of XYZ stock will drop. A short sale is in order. It's the old cliche: Is the glass half-full or half-empty? This variance of opinion, however, is what makes markets work. This chapter will not draw conclusions, but will introduce some of the factors that make up the not-very-exact science of fundamental analysis.

When studying a particular corporation, the fundamental analyst avails himself of the two principal financial reports that corporations publish: *the balance sheet* and the *income statement*. These documents serve two different purposes.

The balance sheet shows the financial condition of a corporation at a given point in time. It lists the *assets*—things of value owned by the corporation—and the *liabilities*—amounts owed by the corporation. The amount by which the assets exceed the liabilities represents the corporation's *net worth*. You could make the same analysis of your personal financial condition. Add your assets—the cash in your pocket and in the bank, the value of securities you own, the value of your house, your car, your stamp collection, and whatever else you own. From this total subtract your liabilities, the losses on your car, the mortgage on your house, your credit card balances, and so on. The difference between your total assets and your total liabilities is equal to your net worth at that moment. It is possible that you might show a negative net worth—many people do. If that is the case, you might be a good short sale.

Corporations do the same thing when they formulate their balance sheet. They generally separate their assets into three categories: current assets, fixed assets and intangible assets.

Current assets are assets that can be converted to cash in one year or less. Such items as marketable securities, accounts receivable, inventory, and cash are considered current assets.

Fixed assets are assets held for use or for investment purposes. They are not expected to be turned into cash in a year or less. Property, buildings, machinery, furniture, and fixtures are among a corporation's fixed assets.

Intangible assets are assets for which an actual value cannot be computed. The corporation might own a patent for a particular product, but what is the patent worth in dollars and cents? The product may become a best-seller and produce millions in sales, but it might also be a failure and never contribute to the corporation's profit. What is a trademark worth? Certainly the Coke trademark used by Coca Cola has worldwide recognition, but what is it worth in dollars? It is really not possible to put a specific value on it. Most corporations assign a modest value to intangible assets. The analyst will beware of a company that she feels overstates these values in order to improve the balance sheet.

Liabilities are separated into two categories: current liabilities and long-term liabilities.

Current liabilities are the opposite of current assets. They consist of obligations that must be paid in one year or less. Such items as accounts payable, taxes payable, interest payable, and current expenses are included in this classification.

Long-term liabilities are liabilities due to be paid in more than one year. The corporation might have mortgage bonds and debentures maturing in ten or fifteen years. While the interest on these bonds for the year is a current liability, the bonds themselves are long-term liabilities.

When the corporation subtracts the total of its liabilities from its total assets, it arrives at the company's net worth. Net worth consists of the stated (par) value of the preferred and common stocks plus the retained earnings. Retained earnings are earnings from prior years of operations. They do not necessarily represent cash, since these earnings may have been used in the conduct of the business.

It is important to understand that the left side of the balance sheet (assets) must be equal to the right side (liabilities + net worth). This is accomplished by making any needed adjustments to the retained earnings.

A corporate balance sheet is subject to much interpretation. The analyst must be able to separate fact from fiction. While financial reports are compiled by competent accountants, these accountants work from information provided by the company management. Therefore, the reputation and past record of management becomes a vital consideration for the fundamental analyst.

Insight into the potential of a corporation and the resulting performance of its stock can be gained from a careful study of the balance sheet. While a thorough study is not possible within a limited approach such as this, some examples of the secrets contained in a balance sheet will be useful.

Working capital is an important factor in a corporation's financial condition, and can be determined by subtracting the current liabilities from the current assets.

Working Capital = Current Assets − Current Liabilities

Working capital is the amount by which the items that can be converted to cash in one year exceed the liabilities that must be paid in one year. A strong working-capital position will enable a company to quickly take advantage of business opportunities. The company will be in a position to acquire other businesses, introduce new products, and expand into new markets. This position can make the company's shares attractive for purchase.

On the other hand a weak working-capital position might attract a short seller's attention, since it could indicate that a company might not be able to keep up with its competitors. The company might find its market share reduced and expansion impossible. If the saying, "It takes money to make money" is true, then the condition of a corporation's working capital is of great interest to the fundamental analyst.

Another determination that can be made from the balance sheet is the makeup of a corporation's capitalization. The capitalization of a company is the total of its long-term debt (bonds) and preferred and common stock (including retained earnings).

If a large portion of a corporation's capitalization is made up of debt securities, the company is said to have a leveraged capitalization.

Leverage has both positive and negative connotations. On the positive side leverage provides the company with tax savings, since interest on bonds is a tax-deductible item while dividends on stocks are paid after taxes. In general the interest cost on bonds is fixed. If bonds are issued with a stated interest rate of 9 percent, that rate will not change during the life of the bond. If the company experiences a series of highly profitable years, the increase in earnings will be more sharply reflected by the common stock. As the common stock makes up a smaller portion of the capitalization of a leveraged corporation, this dramatic earnings increase may result in a price increase for the common shares.

But what happens to a highly leveraged company in bad times? The interest on the debt must still be paid, or bankruptcy can result. Any assets pledged to secure the debt, such as buildings or real estate, can be seized. Leverage, in poor earning periods, can put a company out of business. If an analyst can foresee this as a possibility, a short sale may prove to be profitable.

A company with little or no debt and a large portion of preferred and common stock is said to have a conservative capitalization. In good times the earnings after taxes pass directly to the stockholders, since little or no interest must be paid. The dividend may be increased, and the share price may rise. In poor times an earnings decline may lead to a reduction of the dividend, but not to a cessation of business. Interest on bonds must be paid. Dividends to stockholders are a reward of the company's owners and can be discontinued at any time without resulting in default. Such an action, however, would most probably affect the price of the stock and bring short sellers into the market.

The income statement of a corporation can be compared to an analysis of the financial record of an individual. It consists of three areas of financial details: what the company received for the year, what it spent in the year, and what was left at the end of the year. Income statements can be prepared for shorter periods, such as three or six months, but the one-year reports supply more complete information.

Make up your own income statement. Perhaps last year you took in a total of $75,000 from salary, bonus, interest, dividends, and sale of your used car. You spent $71,000 for rent, food, clothing, entertainment, tuition, loan payments, taxes, interest, and purchase of a new car. Your "bottom line" for the year was $4,000. Of course you could have spent more than you earned and found it necessary to rely on your savings to survive. The same elements are found on a corporate income statement.

In 1991 the XYZ Corporation had total income of $60 million. These funds came from sale of its products, income on its investments, and sale of some property. The corporation dispersed $55 million during the year for raw materials, manufacturing expenses, administrative expenses, taxes, and interest on its bonds.

After all required payments were made, the corporation had $5 million from which to reward its stockholders. It paid a dividend of $1 a share to the owners of the 1 million shares of preferred stock. This payout left $4 million for the common stockholders. If there are 2 million shares of common stock outstanding, this represents earnings of $2 for each common share. Analysts closely watch the trend in earnings as indications of future market action. Both purchase recommendations and short sale recommendations can be triggered by changes in earnings per share. With the $4 million available for common stock holders, the company might elect to pay a dividend of $1 a share on the 2 million shares for a total of $2 million. The remaining $2 million becomes the company bottom line. It represents their retained earnings for the year.

Fundamental analysts carefully study corporate financial reports. In addition, they study government statistics regarding the overall trend of the nation's financial health. Gross national product, institutional output, unemployment statistics, and balance of payments data are just a few items in the seemingly endless flow of information that must be studied. The trend of interest rates must also be watched carefully, since any major changes in rates will certainly be reflected in the market. Buy or sell short? The fundamental analyst constantly seeks the answer to this question.

TECHNICAL ANALYSIS

It would be incorrect to state that the technical analyst ignores fundamental analysis. On the contrary, the technical analyst feels that by studying the trends of prices, the volume of trading, the price patterns, and other statistical data, he can read the results of a corporation's fundamental financial condition. Space limitations do not allow for a complete study of technical analysis, but following are some examples of this market approach that may lead to discussions to buy or to sell short. While some technical analysts employ performance charts and graphs, others employ market theories based on published statistics. We can briefly examine two of these theories.

The Breadth of the Market Theory

The breadth of the market theory is often referred to as the advance decline theory, which is actually more descriptive. The advocate of this theory monitors the stocks that trade on the New York Stock Exchange each day. He totals the number of stocks that advanced, that declined, and that were unchanged in price. There are approximately 1,600 different common stocks that trade on the

Exchange. Although a few of them may not have had any transactions on a given day, the report for a particular day might appear as follows:

Advances	Declines	Unchanged
875	425	200

This indicates that the market is technically strong and higher prices should follow. While it does not measure the potential action of particular securities, it provides an overall market viewpoint that may lead to specific conclusions.

Perhaps the most important application of the breadth of the market theory is its ability to predict a change in the market direction. If the ratio of advances to declines begins to decline, the market, while still strong overall, could be about to reverse its direction. This might be the signal for the short seller to enter the arena. In the example above, the ratio of advances to declines is 2.06 to 1 (875 advances ÷ 425 declines).

A short time later, the trading figures for the day yield the following results:

Advances	Declines	Unchanged
820	510	175

The ratio has now declined to 1.60 to 1 (820 advances ÷ 510 declines). While the number is still positive, the change in the ratio may signal a forthcoming change to negative in the market's direction, and the short seller may seize this opportunity. Naturally, this theory operates in both directions. If declines are outnumbering advances, but the ratio of the difference is becoming smaller, a move to a rising market may well be in the offing. The short seller would cover his positions and take to the sidelines. This is the time for the buyer to step forward.

This explanation of the breadth of the market theory is brief, but it is an example of the use of statistical data to uncover market strengths and weaknesses.

The Short Interest Theory

In general, a short seller becomes active when he foresees a decline in the market. It might then follow that an increase in the number of shares sold short would indicate the likelihood of a falling market, but such is not the case. According to the short interest theory, an increase in short sales is a bullish factor. The existence of a large number of short positions provides a cushion under the market (this theory is often referred to as the cushion theory). Should the market drop, short sellers will begin to cover their short positions, which will help to stem the decline. Their buying will lead others to purchase (create long positions), and a rising market may result. It is also true that no evidence exists that leads to the conclusion that short sellers are any smarter than long buyers. Suppose the short sellers prove to be incorrect, and prices rise rather than fall. At some point the short sellers will be unable or unwilling to finance their short positions and will begin to purchase shares to cover. This will accelerate the rise in prices, and the short seller will be the loser. For these reasons, technical analysts pay close attention to the monthly report that records the current short positions in the various markets. It is published for each security on the major exchange and for stocks that are traded in the over-the-counter market. A figure indicating the overall short position in each market is also made available. Many financial publications will highlight the stocks with the largest short interest and the stocks with the greatest percentage increases and decreases from the previous month.

Figure 8.1 shows a recent monthly report of the short interest on the NYSE. It indicates that as of June 15 the short interest on New York Stock Exchange stocks stood at more than 650 million shares. This number represented a large increase from the previous month, when the total was approximately 644 million shares. At the time of this report, the short interest was at an all-time high.

Figure 8.1 also provides information indicating the stocks with the largest short positions, the largest changes from the prior month, and the stocks with the largest percentage change in their short positions. The analyst watches these changes, as they may

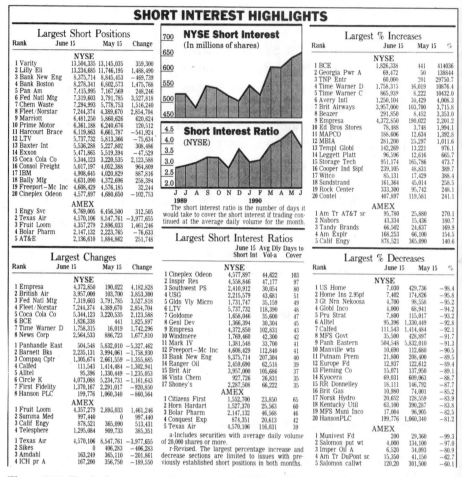

Figure 8.1. Typical summary of major short interest holdings on the New York Stock Exchange from a daily newspaper. (Copyright 1990, The Wall Street Journal. Reproduced by permission.)

lead to decisions to sell short. A large increase in the short position of a particular company might deter the short seller, because that stock now has a large cushion under the current price that lessens the likelihood of a precipitous decline. A reduction in the size of a short position along with the consideration of other elements might encourage the short seller.

The technician following the short interest theory also studies a statistic called the short interest ratio. This figure indicates the number of trading days that will be required to repurchase all of the shares that have been sold short. A short interest ratio of 2.50 would tell us that based on the current volume of trading it will take 2½-days volume to cover all short positions. This is only a measuring device, since all purchases of stocks are not made to cover shorts, but it enables one to analyze the short interest from a different viewpoint. Followers of this theory feel that a ratio in excess of 3.00 is a bullish indication. At the time of publication of Figure 8.1, the ratio stood at 3.86.

The theorist would consider this a signal of a rising market, and short sales may not be in order. The ratio in the month prior to that in Figure 8.1 was 4.61, substantially larger than the current figure's ratio. How could the ratio decline while the total short interest increased? The reason can be traced to an increase in the volume of trading. Although the size of short positions grew, the volume in the market also rose. While there are more shares sold short than in the prior months, the number of days needed to cover these positions would be less due to an increase in market activity.

The short interest ratio can be applied to individual stocks and to the general market. Simply divide the short position in the stock by the average daily volume of trading. This formula can be useful in determining the propriety of a short sale.

Decisions, however, should not be based on a single factor. An increased short position, while technically considered to be bullish, might have been caused by a fundamentally sound event. A company might have declared bankruptcy, its major product might have been found to cause an incurable disease, or the company's president might even have been indicted for robbing the corporate treasury. Use this data as a tool in your investment planning, but also employ other tools. One method seldom is sufficient. You cannot build a doghouse with only a hammer; you might need some nails.

The short interest theory also bears further study. Not all short sales are made in the anticipation of a market decline. Some are made for reasons discussed earlier, such as deferring taxes or arbitrage. In these cases the short position will not be covered by purchasing the stock and therefore will not be part of the cushion under the current price. The person who sells short to defer her tax liability until next year will simply wait until after the calendar turns to January and deliver the stock that she has owned all along. No purchase will be made. The arbitrageur simply looks for a disparity in prices that may provide a possibility of profit.

For example, XYZ Corporation has outstanding an issue of convertible bonds. Each $1,000 bond can be exchanged for 50 shares of the company's stock, at the option of the bondholder. At a given point these convertible bonds are trading at a price of 90 ($900). Since each bond is convertible into 50 shares of the stock, the comparable value of the stock would be $18 a share:

$$\text{Bond value: } \$900 \div 50 \text{ shares} = \$18$$

Suppose the stock is actually trading at $19 a share. The arbitrageur will move quickly. He will buy the bond at 90 ($900) and sell 50 shares of the stock short at $19 ($950). He has made a profit of $50. The short sale, however, will not be covered by a purchase of the stock. The arbitrageur will simply convert the bond and deliver the shares he received against the short.

The figures provided each month regarding the short interest cannot be evaluated without further analysis. Since our markets have grown, other market devices can be used to accomplish much the same results as those expected from short selling. The presence of options and futures, for example, have brought permanent changes in the way business is conducted. The thorough analyst employs many tools in arriving at market decisions.

CHART PATTERNS

The chartist records the past price performance of a single stock or of the market in general. By properly reading the events of the past, he feels that future movement can be accurately predicted. In addition to price movements, he may often consider the accompanying volume of trading. An upward or downward movement that occurs with a small volume of trading is not as significant as one in which the volume is inordinately large.

Some market observers consider charts to be the ultimate measurement of market behavior. They may totally disdain the fundamentals and rely completely on the moving lines on their charts. Others relegate chartists to the status of a strange cult whose ideas are without foundation, but who must be tolerated simply because they exist. Charts are either loved or hated; there seems to be no in-between. Compare charts to a Sunday dinner of calf's liver and bacon smothered with onions. Serve this meal to one guest, and he will become your friend for life. But another guest will immediately leave the room, perhaps even the country, to avoid exposure to this vile-smelling, evil-tasting substitute for real food. Marriages have been dissolved due to liver, bacon, and onions. Charts can also lead to divorce.

One factor regarding charts that even the most cynical critic cannot deny is that they are often self-serving. If a large number of technical analysts believe that a stock will suffer a severe decline if a particular price is reached, the result will be as predicted. When that price is reached, the analysts receive the same signal and begin to sell; the price then declines. If a buy signal is given, the purchase orders pour in from the chart followers; up goes the stock as expected. Although the resulting price movement may be temporary and may quickly reverse itself, the prediction for the moment has come true.

The study of chart techniques is no simple matter. There are scores of textbooks completely devoted to this subject. This text will make no attempt to emulate these writings but instead will give just a few simple examples of the interpretation of chart patterns. These patterns are a major factor in the decisions of short sellers and therefore cannot be ignored.

Support and Resistance Levels

Most charts use a moving line to record the price movement of a security over a period of time. The price is measured vertically and the time period, horizontally. In some cases the record shows that a particular stock has declined to a specific level on a number of occasions. Each time this level is reached, buyers enter the market and a rise in price follows. This price is called a *support level*. If the price is reached again, the chartist anticipates that buyers will again arrive and force the price higher. The chartist becomes a buyer at

Figure 8.2. Price chart for a hypothetical stock illustrating a price support level of 50.

that price. However, if the support level is penetrated, the stock must find new support at a lower price. The seller, including the short seller, now places his orders.

In other instances a stock is unable to continue a rising trend above a certain price. Each time the price is reached, orders to sell the stock appear and the decline occurs. This is known as a *resistance level*. If that price is touched again, short sales might prove rewarding. But beware. If the resistance level is penetrated the stock might reach still higher prices, and buyers rather than short sellers will profit at this price.

Figures 8.2 and 8.3 illustrate support and resistance levels for hypothetical stocks.

Head and Shoulders Patterns

Figure 8.4 illustrates a pattern known as a head and shoulders pattern. The price of a stock has risen from a base to a higher level (left shoulder) before retreating again to approximately the same

Figure 8.3. Price chart for a hypothetical stock illustrating a price resistance level of 80.

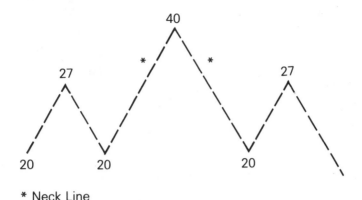

Figure 8.4. Price chart for a hypothetical stock illustrating a bearish head and shoulder pattern.

base point. This rise and drop is followed by a rise to a still-higher price (head) and then by a retreat to the base. A third rally carries the price to a point equal to the first rally (right shoulder), but again the stock price declines. If this fall in price penetrates the base, the stock will suffer a further serious decline. A short seller should consider entering the market as the price declines near the base for the third time. If the base is penetrated, he should profit. If the stock rallies, he will cover his position.

Figure 8.5 illustrates an inverted head and shoulders. The interpretation is the same but in this case is bullish. Short sellers should take to the sidelines. It is the buyers' turn.

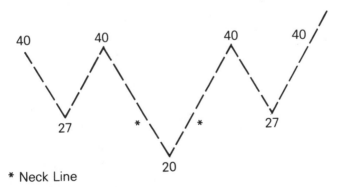

Figure 8.5. Price chart for a hypothetical stock illustrating a bullish inverted head and shoulder pattern.

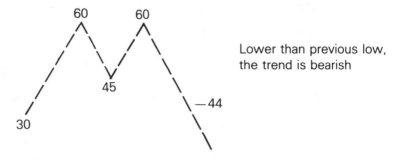

Figure 8.6. Price chart for a hypothetical stock illustrating a bearish M pattern.

M and W Patterns

M and W patterns have similarities to the previously discussed support and resistance level formations, but they may occur over shorter time periods.

An M pattern is bearish and attracts short sellers who rely on this technical approach. With this pattern, the price of the stock being followed rises to a certain level, but then meets resistance and declines. It rallies again, meets resistance again at the same approximate price, and retreats. If the second decline brings the price to a point lower than the first decline, the M pattern has been completed and a further drop in value will occur. The short seller enters the game. A W pattern is the opposite of the M pattern, and if completed provides a bullish forecast. Figures 8.6 and 8.7 provide simple illustrations of these patterns.

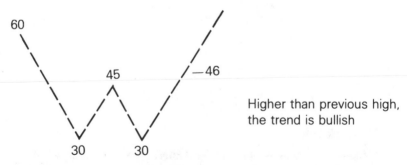

Figure 8.7. Price chart for a hypothetical stock illustrating a bullish W pattern.

The analysis of securities is serious business. Many fortunes have been made and lost due to actions based on market analysis. We have briefly described some of the elements of the two principal analytical areas—fundamental and technical—and a few unorthodox market theories that have also claimed some followers. Investors should devote some study to the evaluation of securities markets and trends. Often, no amount of study will shield you from market movements. Unfavorable economic news can precipitate a general decline, which will affect even the strongest companies; owners of almost all stocks will suffer. Unexpected good news will bring rising prices, which may carry along even those stocks that are fundamentally or technically unsound; the hard-working short seller will be wearing a frown.

The intent here is not to recommend a particular method of analysis as a road to success. Even the experts disagree. If they did not, there would be no market at all. The market cannot have everyone wishing to buy. There must be someone to disagree and therefore to sell.

Select the approach that suits you best or that is recommended to you by a professional whom you trust. No single system provides the optimum result. A story is told that not long ago there was a man who had worked on Wall Street for more than twenty years. His career had been fulfilling, but not overly rewarding from a financial standpoint. His true love was thoroughbred horse racing. At every opportunity he would frequent the racetracks in the New York City area and even used his vacation for an annual August trip to the meeting at Saratoga Springs. But the man very seldom placed a wager. According to his system, he placed bets only on thoroughbreds that met each of the following three criteria:

1. The horse must be gray in color.
2. The name of the horse must end in a vowel.
3. The silks worn by the jockey must include the color green or yellow (preferably both).

Since very few horses met those difficult standards, he placed very few bets; but that was his system. This man has not been seen of late. Perhaps he is staying at his condominium in Bermuda or his ranch in Colorado, both purchased with his racetrack winnings.

9

Commodity Futures

Before commodity futures can be discussed as instruments for the short seller, each term must first be defined separately. A *commodity* is something that is useful or of value. A *future* is a contract calling for delivery of a commodity at a later date, according to the specific details of the agreement.

It is important to understand the difference between an options contract and a futures contract. If you purchase a call on General Motors stock that expires next January and has an exercise price of $80 a share, you have the privilege, but not the obligation, to exercise the contract. If General Motors stock is trading lower than $80 a share, you will probably allow the contract to expire and your only loss will be the premium paid for the call.

Not so with futures contracts. If you purchase a futures contract for corn at $2.90 a bushel with January delivery, you have entered into an entirely different form of agreement. If you do not offset your position by selling the contract or by purchasing a similar contract before January, 5,000 bushels of corn will be delivered to you and you will be expected to pay $2.90 per bushel. If you live in a small apartment on the East Side of Manhattan, this could lead to a problem of logistics.

Futures contracts are traded on a number of different exchanges in the United States. Among them are the Chicago Board of Trade, the Chicago Mercantile Exchange, the Kansas City Board of Trade, and the Commodity Exchange Inc. (NYC). Since the early trading of commodities was primarily based on agricultural products and livestock, the midwestern part of the country, where these products originated, dominated the markets. In today's trading, futures contracts are available in a wide variety of products, ranging from currencies to soybeans. Some examples of the commodities on which contracts are available for trading are listed would include:

Livestock
  Cattle
  Hogs
  Pork bellies

Foods and Fiber
  Cocoa
  Coffee
  Cotton
  Orange juice
  Sugar

Grains
  Corn
  Oats
  Soybeans
  Wheat

Industrial Products
  Crude oil
  Heating oil
  Gasoline

Metals
  Copper
  Gold
  Palladium
  Platinum
  Silver

Currencies
  British pound
  Canadian dollars
  Japanese yen
  Swiss franc
  German mark

Financial Instruments
  U.S. Treasury bills
  U.S. Treasury notes
  U.S. Treasury bonds
  Eurodollar deposits

Futures on stock indexes such as the Standard & Poor's 500 Stock Index are also available for trading. These contracts are dealt with somewhat differently and have unique applications in our markets. A discussion of stock index futures will be presented in the next chapter.

Just as with options, the terms of commodity contracts are established by the exchanges on which they are traded. Unlike options, however, commodity contracts differ greatly, depending on the product underlying the contract. While options contracts generally represent 100 shares of stock, a commodity contract can represent a varied quantity of the product. For example, a sugar contract represents 112,000 pounds; a cotton contract, 50,000 pounds; a corn contract, 5,000 bushels; and a futures contract for gold, 100 troy ounces.

Another variable is the minimum permissible price fluctuation for a particular contract. Options are generally traded in variations of ¼ of $1 ($0.25), just as in stocks. In futures the price variations differ for particular contracts. For example, gold contracts are traded at $0.10 per troy ounce; cattle, at $0.025 a pound; and wheat, at $0.0025 per bushel.

The price of a futures contract can also be expressed in a number of ways. A price of 2.90 for a corn contract indicates dollars per bushel. In this case it represents $2.90 for each of the 5,000 bushels in the contract. Contracts for gasoline are priced in cents per gallon. Thus a price of 56.12 on one of these contracts represents $0.5612 cents for each of the 42,000 gallons included in each contract.

Futures contracts are also traded with many different expiration months. The number of months varies with each particular contract, but some contracts run as long as a year and a half into the future.

The spot, or cash market, for commodities indicates contracts made for immediate delivery of the product. The current expiration month for contracts is also deemed to be part of the spot market.

The major difference in the trading of futures contracts as opposed to other products is the imposition of limits on the price fluctuation on a given day. The limit up or limit down varies with each underlying product and eliminates the possibility of extremely large price changes on a given trading day. The limit also reduces the marketability of the contracts, since a seller may be unable to reduce his position if a contract is already limit down for the day. The same problem will face a (potential) buyer in a limit up situation. Certainly this trading technique leads to more orderly markets, but it does so at the expense of marketability. The investor in common stocks can always buy or sell. She may not like the price, but with rare exceptions (such as occurred with the sudden death of President John Fitzgerald Kennedy) the market is always there to serve her. On Monday, October 19, 1987, the most violent decline in our history occurred. Some stocks lost more than 20 percent of their value, but the market still permitted people to sell if they wished. The same is not true with the futures markets. The imposed limits control daily price fluctuations. This is not to favor one system over the other; they both have positives and negatives. But they are certainly different, and traders must be fully aware of the restrictions that the differences cause. The limits vary, as stated above, depending on the product and the dollar value of the contract. For example, the daily limit for corn is $0.10 a bushel, while the soybean contract can rise or fall as much as $0.30 a bushel. The various limits can be found in any standard futures text but are subject to frequent change by the exchanges.

SHORT SELLING FUTURES

The applications of futures contracts are the same as those for other investment vehicles. They can be used for speculation or for protecting other positions. The short seller is quite active in futures markets and utilizes his strategies for both of these purposes. By looking at a few examples of the short seller as a speculator in commodity futures, potential rewards and possible risks can be analyzed.

What is the most unreliable item of information transmitted by the media? You may disagree, but it is the weather forecast. How often have you planned a weekend at the seashore based on the forecast of clear and sunny skies? When you arrive at your cramped cottage on Friday night, the clouds begin to empty themselves onto the entire area. The deluge does end—late on Sunday afternoon as you are packing the car for the return trip. So you have spent two days indoors trying to amuse the children with crayons and coloring books! Of course it may work the other way. The experts predict a stormy weekend, and you cancel a planned golf or tennis game. Naturally the sun shines continually, and a refreshing breeze blows while you sit indoors reading the newest bestseller, *The Lives and Loves of the Roving Bison*.

Weather greatly affects the value of many commodity futures contracts, particularly grains. For instance, a healthy rain during the growing season will lead to a larger-than-expected crop. The excess supply will result in lower prices and will attract the short seller. Recently the following headline appeared in the financial press: "Corn and Soybean Prices Fall after Forecast of Rain."

On this day the futures prices of corn and soybeans, as well as wheat and oats, dropped sharply. The weather forecast, however, must be accurate. To obtain this commodity, traders often rely on a much more reliable system than the usual media sources. This system is called the family. Early each morning the grain trader calls Mom and Dad in Iowa, Aunt Kate in Nebraska, Cousin Arnold in Kansas, and Uncle Jake in Illinois. Based on their forecasts, the trader takes his position. These people are never wrong about the weather. They live off the land and can read each of nature's signals; they are the backbone of America; they are working farmers. While this may sound foolish, it is nonetheless true. If you travel to Chicago, try to meet some grain traders. They will verify this method of market analysis, which probably works as well as any other. Obviously poor weather may shrink crops and force prices higher. Short sellers will most likely cover any existing positions and take no new ones.

The futures market also deals in contracts in foreign currency. They are similar to currency options, with one important variation. An options contract may never be exercised; the choice is up to the holder of the option. A futures contract, however, calls for delivery of the commodity during a given future month.

One contract that is traded is based on the German mark. Each contract represents 125,000 units of that currency. A speculator might envision lower values for the mark when compared to the U.S. dollar. Perhaps she believes that the problems of German reunification may place a strain on the economy and reduce the value of the mark. In this case she may sell short futures contracts at the then-current price of 0.6025 ($0.6025 per mark). The value of each contract is $75,312.50 (125,000 marks × $0.6025). If she is correct and the value of the mark drops to 0.5900 ($0.59 per mark), she may cover her short position at that price. Her cost would be 73,750.00 (125,000 marks × $0.59), giving her a profit (less expenses) of $1,562.50 for each contract. Rather than repurchase the contract, she can choose to purchase marks in the cash market to deliver against her contract. In either case, she will profit, but a loss is also a possibility. If the mark increases in value, she will either have to cover her position by buying back the contract or purchase the currency in the market for delivery. In either case, a loss will result.

The futures market offers almost unlimited speculation opportunities for the short seller. Is the Soviet Union, the world's largest producer of gold, about to sell large quantities of the metal to raise hard currency for its economic reform? Such action would surely drive down the price and with it the value of the futures contracts. Has the surgeon general of the United States announced that some particular grain is hazardous to your health? (Almost everything is, it seems.) If a futures contract for this grain is traded in the market, a short seller may enter his orders.

HEDGING WITH FUTURES

While speculators participate in the futures market in hopes of making short-term profits, they also assist the more conservative market participants by offsetting their trading activities. Conservative commodities players often use these markets to hedge positions and to guarantee prices on products that they may require in the future.

Many industrial companies require particular commodities for production of their products. For example, manufacturers such as Eastman Kodak use large amounts of silver in their business. Futures contracts for silver trade on both the Commodity Exchange in New York (COMEX) and the Chicago Board of Trade (CBT). The COMEX contract represents 5,000 troy ounces of the metal and is valued in cents per ounce. A price of 490.00 is equivalent to $4.90 an ounce. In its production planning, Eastman Kodak may consider this price to be within its cost analysis. Metal purchased at this price can be converted to products that will be sold later at a profit. The company might fill its anticipated needs by purchasing futures contracts that supply it with the necessary raw material. The company eliminates the risk of rising prices in later months and locks in an important element of its production costs. Since industrial buyers will generally deal in large quantities, their activity can lead to a rise in price, but this may also present an opportunity for the short seller. In any financial product—stocks, bonds, options, or commodities—a predominance of buyers leads to higher prices. When the buyers are finished, however, the market usually declines. The short seller, aware of this market axiom, supplies the buyer by selling contracts at continually rising prices. When the buying slows and the market reacts downward, he hopes to cover his short position profitably. Short-term traders, both buyers and sellers, often take the opposite side of a market trend. When this trend reverses they profit. But the short seller of the silver also assisted the buyer. Had the short seller not been present in the marketplace, the buyer might have been forced to pay higher prices. In addition, when the short seller covers his positions by becoming a buyer, he accommodates those who sell to him. As stated earlier, you may never consider selling short yourself, but your market activities will often be affected by those who do use this trading technique.

Suppose a farmer makes his living by raising hogs. Although it may be many months before his animals are ready for market, he will closely watch the commodities futures market. It may allow him to protect himself against loss or even help him ensure a profit.

The Chicago Mercantile Exchange (CME) lists a futures contract for live hogs. The contract calls for delivery of 30,000 pounds of hogs and trades in cents per pound. At a given point, the value of the contract is 0.6190 ($0.619 per pound). The hog raiser has computed that at this price he will show a reasonable profit for his animals. He can wait and hope that the price will rise, but he may be content to lock in the current price. He would sell short the appropriate numbers of futures contracts. If at the time of delivery the price has risen to 0.6310 ($0.631 per pound), he has two choices: he can deliver his product at the contract price of 0.6190 which, while lower than the current price, still leaves him with a profit, or he might also choose to repurchase the contract at a loss and sell his hogs at the higher price now available. His main benefit by shorting the futures contracts lies in the possibility of protecting himself against a falling price. By delivery date the price might be 0.594 ($0.594 per pound). At this price, he would have a loss after months of hard work, but this dire fate will not befall him. His contract allows him to deliver at $0.619 a pound. His entry into the commodities futures market has saved the day.

Do not overlook the risks to which the short seller is always subject. Suppose some unforeseeable event occurs that destroys the hogs—blight, disease, or natural disaster. At delivery time the hogs are not available. The hog raiser had contracted to deliver at $0.619 a pound and cannot. Therefore he will be required to repurchase the contract. Due to the shortage the price might now be $0.640 a pound. His loss will be drastic and perhaps unrecoverable.

What can be done by the raiser of hogs can also be done by the wheat farmer, the oil refiner, or the producer of any product that is the subject of a commodities futures contract. They can sell short at today's price and deliver at a later date. The short sale can prevent loss and perhaps ensure profit, but they must be able to deliver. If any event occurs that prevents proper delivery, the loss can be staggering.

A businessman in Dallas has sold a large order of cowboy boots to a Swiss client. He will be paid on delivery (in three months) in Swiss francs. At the time of the sale, the Swiss franc is valued at $0.71. Our manufacturer in Texas has computed his profit based on that figure. The total value of the shipment is about $355,000 or about 500,000 Swiss francs at the $0.71 value (500,000 × $0.71 = $355,000). Delivery, however, will not be made for three months. Suppose in that time the value of the Swiss franc is down to $0.68. When the Dallas businessman receives his 500,000 Swiss francs, the U.S. value will be only $340,000. He has received the agreed number of francs, but his true profit has been reduced by $15,000. He might use the futures market to protect himself.

The International Monetary Market (IMM) in Chicago trades a futures contract in Swiss francs. Each contract represents 125,000 francs. The businessman sells four contracts (500,000 francs) at a price of $0.71. Since he does not have the francs at this time, the sale is considered a short sale. Three months later he receives payment for his goods and uses the Swiss currency to complete delivery on his futures contracts. If the franc value is higher, say $0.72, he will have sacrificed some additional profit. But he is not in the business of speculating in foreign currencies. He manufactures cowboy boots. He had a profit at the $0.71 value and was not looking for more. He just did not want to risk losing all or a major part of his profit. The futures market provided an alternative.

Again the risk must be recognized. Suppose the buyer in Switzerland goes out of business and does not complete his side of the contract. Not only does the man in Dallas still have the boots, he is short 500,000 Swiss francs at $0.71. He must either buy back the contract or purchase the francs in the cash market for delivery. In either case a loss of great magnitude can occur. The short seller is the true daredevil of the marketplace. In even the most conservative applications, the risks of short selling are large and perhaps unlimited. The buyer of a security or commodity can only lose the amount of the investment. The short seller has no such assurance.

In trading futures, as with options, an important statistic that must be considered is the *open interest*. This figure indicates the number of contracts for a particular product that remain outstanding at a given point in time. The open interest can be measured as a total for a particular commodity or can be broken down into each expiration month. As all open contracts must eventually be closed out either by delivery or by repurchase the open interest becomes of great importance to the trader. If the open interest is large, any decline in value for the contract may induce purchase to cover open positions. This action adds support to a declining market. A small open interest deprives the market of this support and may cause declines to become more severe. On the other hand a large open interest is tantamount to a large short position in a stock. A rise in the market may force short sellers to cover purchases and may accelerate the upward momentum. Traders, including short sellers, pay close attention to these figures, and any changes motivate market action.

Commodity futures, just like stocks, can be purchased on margin. But unlike stocks, where the initial margin is 50 percent of the cost of the purchase, the initial margin on futures is generally only 5 percent or 10 percent of the contract value. The actual margin tends to be higher for speculators than for users (hedgers). This difference has both positive and negative connotations. While it allows a trader to acquire large positions with a minimal cash outlay, it also can result in a rapid evaporation of equity, which will lead to calls for more margin to be deposited. This may force the trader to liquidate his position. Remember, unlike stocks, a future may be down the limit for the day, thereby precluding further sales. The margin requirements vary from contract to contract and are established by the exchange on which each commodity trades. Brokerage firms often impose their own requirements to protect themselves against loss. These "house" requirements may be substantially higher than those set down by the exchanges.

THE FUTURE OF FUTURES

The use of commodity futures as a market instrument has increased greatly in recent decades. Originally they were designed to allow for speculation in grain, crops, and livestock, and to help producers of these products reduce their risk by hedging inventory. In today's market, commodities futures have been expanded to include contracts on financial instruments, precious metals, currencies, and indexes.

Participants in the market have grown in direct proportion to the increase of available products. This growth should continue into the future as markets become more and more international. Both the short seller and the buyer, however, will always be there waiting for their opportunities.

10

Stock Index Futures and Program Trading

Stock index futures deserve a special study. Since their introduction in 1982, they have become one of the most actively traded products in the futures markets. Although it bears some similarities to index options, the index future is unique in both its trading mechanisms and its applications. While contracts are available on many indexes, the example used here is the most popular one—the Standard & Poor's 500 Stock Index. The S&P 500 is traded on the Chicago Mercantile Exchange (CME).

An index is an instrument used to trace the price movement of a large group of stocks. It provides a more accurate reading of general market trends than would the record of the price changes in a single stock. Traditionally, indexes were used only as a measuring device; the index itself was not a trading vehicle. With the introduction of options trading on exchanges, options on indexes became available. But the purchaser of an index option does not buy the component parts of the index; he simply purchases an option on the index with a specific strike price. For this he pays a premium. At expiration of the option, the holder can exercise his option and be paid the difference between his strike price and the current market value in cash. If the option has no value, he just allows it to expire and loses only the premium.

With an index future the procedure is different. The buyer purchases the index at its current level and deposits the required margin. At expiration the futures contract is settled, again in cash, based on the difference between original contract price and then-current value. Should the holder of the future not wish to settle, he must sell the contract, probably at a loss, and eliminate the position. The original seller of the index future has the same choice. He can allow the contract to settle, or he can cover his position by purchasing a similar contract. With index futures the client actually purchases or sells an interest in the 500 stocks included in the index. The purchase or sale is based on a mathematical model of the value of the futures contract. He does not actually buy or sell 500 different stocks, but the privilege received and risks undertaken are quite the same as if he had done so. There is no premium involved.

To determine the total value of an index future, a predetermined multiplier is used. The multiplier for the S&P 500 index future is 500. The multiplier is applied to the current dollar value of the index to arrive at the overall dollar amount involved.

On a given day, the financial page provides the following information:

S&P 500 - Closing Price 365.40

On that day the total value of this index future was $182,700 ($365.40 × 500).

A trader who anticipated a rise in the general market could purchase one or more of these contracts and deposit the required margin. The margin on index futures is relatively small, allowing large dollar values to be traded with only a minor commitment of cash. These requirements will be discussed later in this chapter. The bear, believing a market decline to be imminent, may sell this contract short.

Although most traders in index futures close out their positions prior to expiration, suppose that in this example the contract is allowed to run its course. At that point the contract will be settled in cash, and there will be one winner and one loser. In effect, it is a "zero-sum game."

At expiration, the S&P 500 is valued at 372.80. This translates into $186,400 (372.80 × $500). The buyer at 365.40 has a profit of $3,700 on each contract ($186,400 − $182,700). The seller, of course, has an identical loss. However, had the value at expiration been 362.30, the seller would show the profit (362.30 × $500 = $181,150 per contract). The seller's profit upon settlement is $1,550 for each contract ($182,700 − $181,150).

In each case, the trader was able to participate in a large segment of the market, rather than being forced to select a small number of stocks that would perform as desired. The trader also was able to take his position for a minimal outlay of cash.

As noted earlier, the purchaser of stocks on margin must deposit 50 percent of the cost of securities as an initial requirement. He then borrows the balance from his broker and pays interest on the loan. The short seller of stock must also deposit a minimum of 50 percent of the proceeds of the sale. The trader in stock index futures is faced with much lower requirements. Although the exchanges alter the percentage required frequently, the figures in use as of this writing will be used here. Actually, the margin requirements are different for the two categories of traders. Professional traders and hedgers have one requirement, while speculators have a higher one.

A speculator purchasing one S&P 500 index future would have to deposit approximately 12 percent. Using the example of the purchase of a contract at 365.40, for an aggregate price of $182,700, the speculator's initial requirement would be about $21,924. The buyer of the actual stock included in this index would have to deposit $91,350 (50 percent of $182,700).

The professional trader would have to deposit even less cash, currently only about 5 percent. The $182,700 of underlying security value could be bought with the deposit of only about $9,135. This is one tenth of the amount demanded from the buyer of these same stocks in a margin account.

INDEX FUTURES AND THE INSTITUTIONAL INVESTOR

Index futures became a very popular product immediately after their introduction. At first, the applications were quite simple. The bull or the bear could take a large position in the market with a minimal outlay of cash. A professional trader might buy or sell one contract in the example given earlier with a deposit of only $9,135. Since each 1-point move represents a value change of $5000, his reward, if he was correct, could be quite dramatic. As the values change continually, he might cover his long or short positions at a 2-point gain on the same day, resulting in a gross profit of $1,000 on a $9,135 investment, or more than 10 percent. This is not bad at all.

Before long, institutional investors recognized the potential in the trading of index futures. Futures could be used to establish positions or to protect existing ones. (They could also be applied in such a way as to relieve the money manager of the burden of making decisions, although few, if any, quality professionals would accept such shortcuts.)

A professional investment manager, such as a pension fund or university endowment manager, foresees a rising stock market. She would like to participate, but is temporarily short of cash. Payments into these investment funds is often made on specific dates during the year, and her next influx of dollars is not due for three months. She can enter the market by buying index futures. For a limited cash outlay, she can buy contracts representing 500 stocks of major corporations. As they rise in value, so will the futures and the profits will accrue. She may be able to acquire even larger positions using futures than she would have been able to by buying the actual securities. As a further advantage, the expenses involved in purchasing the futures are likely to be less than those related to trading stocks. Were she to buy 50 or 100 different stocks, she would be charged a commission on each trade by the broker handling the orders. With futures, she pays one commission and receives an interest in 500 stocks. There are, of course, some drawbacks. The futures contract will expire in time, and she will have either a gain or a loss. A holding in the underlying stocks includes no such restrictions. Also, if the institution owned the stocks, they would receive dividends. Futures contracts do not pay dividends. If the client requires current income, index futures will not provide the answer. But they do afford the opportunity to acquire, or sell, a broad stock position with a limited cash outlay.

The manager of another large stock portfolio is faced with quite a different dilemma. His market analysis has led to the conclusion that a major market decline is in the offing. Should he liquidate all of the holdings in advance of the decline? To do so would present serious problems. To sell a large number of shares is costly. The broker handling the orders will charge the client a commission which may appear small when measured on a per share basis but would add up to a major expense when a great number of shares are sold. It is also quite obvious that once the shares are sold, they are no longer owned. Hence, no dividends will be received, thereby depriving the fund of the income. Although the funds received could be invested elsewhere, the result may not be as satisfying. Most important, the market expert is convinced that the fall in the market will be only a temporary reversal. He does not want to eliminate the entire portfolio now and then scramble to reassemble it later. Index futures can come to the rescue!

The portfolio manager sells short a sufficient number of S&P 500 contracts to replicate the value of the stocks held by the client. For example, if the portfolio has a value of $10 million and each S&P 500 contract has underlying value of $197,000, he would sell short 50 futures contracts, representing a total value of $9,850,000. As the market drops, so will the value of the futures contracts. The variety of stocks in the futures contract should cause its performance to be similar to that of the shares in the client's portfolio. Any loss in the $10 million portfolio should be offset by the profits achieved by selling the S&P 500 short. The costs will be less than selling the shares, and the dividends will continue to roll in. In this case, the short sale was used in a conservative manner. It was not used to speculate, but to protect a large but vulnerable position.

Index futures contracts can also be used as a substitute for market analysis. If you were charged with the management of a large sum of money intended to be invested in common stocks, you would be faced with many decisions. You would be required to apply a lot of time to the analysis of the publicly traded securities to select those most promising for your clients. After months of studying financial statements, technical charts, and economic reports, you select the shares of 100 companies. But they all go down, while most everything goes up. Or perhaps some of your selections rise, but the overall increase for the year is only 7 percent. Your phone begins to ring and the clients' complaints all sound the same. "The market was up 16 percent last year, but your recommendations are only up 7 percent. You're not doing your job!" What do they mean by the "market"? Usually, they are referring to the general movement of common stocks as measured by some popular average or index, such as Dow Jones or Standard & Poor's. Why fight it? Just buy all of the stocks included in, for example, the S&P 500 index. If that index is up 16 percent, so too will be your portfolio. Then when the phone rings, you are prepared: "Our performance equaled that of the prestigious S&P 500 stock index. We are very proud of our record. If the S&P goes down, you can say, quite truthfully, that you did no worse than those world-famous experts at S&P who selected the stocks used in the index.

In fact, why bother to buy all of those stocks? Just buy a sufficient number of S&P 500 stock index futures. The result will be lower cost, less expense, and certainly a simplification of your duties. No longer will you be forced to spend your time interpreting balance sheets and reading charts and government economic reports. Your reading time will be free for more enjoyable works, such as those authored by Jack Higgins, Judith Krantz, Dick Francis, and Dave Barry.

When the future of the market looks dark, you can hedge your position by selling index futures short. This approach to investing has become quite popular. Those practicing this method simply strive to do no better or worse than the market in general. They avoid making selections themselves, but pass that task along to those who select the components of the indexes. Forget that the indexes are not meant to be recommendations. They are to measure, not to suggest. The practitioner has found a new use for an old product.

By merely following the index stocks, the manager has achieved what in today's world is the equivalent of success. He has achieved mediocrity.

PROGRAM TRADING

Although index futures have been popular since their introduction in 1982, the true growth of the device began when the futures were combined with the actual market for stocks to implement programs dictated by a computer.

Computerized trading and its offspring *program trading,* have been the major topic of discussion and debate in the securities industry for many years. Some participants see them as necessary; others call for their banishment. Computer trading programs have been blamed for everything from the market crashes of October 1987 and October 1989 to the crash of the New York Yankees in 1990.

How often have you seen a headline such as this, which recently appeared in a financial publication: "Dow Falls 23.27 in Heavy Program Trading." All investors must have some understanding of this market strategy. As with other strategies, you may never apply it to your own investing, but you must know what it is. It affects the market, and you as well, on a daily basis. It is particularly pertinent to this discussion since short selling plays a major role in computerized trading.

In the early 1980s major institutional clients, such as pension funds, universities, and investment companies, with the assistance of some large brokerage firms, sought to apply the advances in modern computer technology to the art of timing investments. Using a variety of sophisticated systems, they created computerized programs that emitted signals when the market level indicated that the time to buy or sell had arrived. Speed was important as each player knew that many others were seeking the same signal. Whoever got there first usually executed orders at the best prices.

In the beginning, the placement of orders was done manually. As it was not known beforehand whether the signal would indicate buy or sell, the brokers handling the orders prepared for either event. It was not uncommon to see order clerks on the floor of the New York Stock Exchange guarding two cigar boxes of prepared orders. Using the key stocks traded in the market, one box contained buy orders and the other sell orders for the same amount of the same securities. When the machine gave the buy signal, a quick call to the floor would instruct the clerk to "execute the white box," the one containing the buy orders. When the computer said sell, the clerk would be told to "execute the red box," the cigarless container holding the sell orders. In either situation, orders to buy or sell vast amounts of particular stock would flood the trading post at which dealings in these shares took place.

As these programs often coincided in their decisions, it was not one program but many that led to the same buy or sell instructions. The effect on the price of each stock, as well as on the total market, was radical. Because these programs usually operated in the last hour or less of the day's trading, the closing market level often reflected only these "last-minute" transactions, rather than the history of the entire day. The last hour became the province of the professional trader. Although the Exchange closes at 4:00 P.M. eastern standard time, one very astute market observer stated that "the individual investor should consider that the market ends each day at 3:00 P.M. That last hour is not his. It belongs to the professional traders and speculators."

Once the programs kicked in, sending the market into an upward or downward spiral, others joined in. Even those without computers could read the trend once it had begun, and once they followed the lead, they increased the magnitude of the rise or fall. Short sellers actively participated in down markets by attempting to predict their occurrence. They also tried to gauge the end of a computer-driven rise in prices. Short sales made as the rally began to weaken usually proved profitable. But what about the small investor who was part of the programs? She could find her holdings down in value by 3 points a share with no explanation other than the familiar headlines: "Market Sharply Lower due to Program Trading."

As the time passed, the ability to execute the program orders became greatly simplified. Those cigar boxes were pretty cumbersome; once more, technology came to the fore. The Exchange introduced a system called *designated order turnaround* (DOT), which allows orders for up to 2,099 shares to be executed automatically through a computer. The big brother of DOT, called super DOT, goes even further and can supply computerized execution of orders as large as 30,900 shares if they are entered prior to the opening of the market. These systems, which are available to brokers, can also be provided to clients, allowing almost instantaneous execution of computer-driven orders.

The slide (or rise) begins and may drive prices down to unrealistic levels when basic financial factors regarding the particular stocks are considered. But it must be remembered that the orders initiated by the computer may improve the client's performance. This is what the broker is paid to do. Certainly, the orders create commissions for the brokers handling the trades, and they would be unlikely to reject this largess. Many major brokerage firms, such as Morgan Stanley, Salomon Brothers, and Jeffries & Co., have even developed electronic systems that they will make available to clients. These firms want the orders that the system will generate. Who can blame them? This is their business.

PROGRAM TRADING AND CRASHES

Did this computerized trading cause the October market crashes in 1987 and 1989? Can it lead to future incidents of the same or greater magnitude? While many experts will answer these questions yes, an equal number would probably reply with a no. But whether computerized trading causes inordinate market rises or falls, it most certainly can contribute to their severity. A market begins to decline for some unrelated reason, and the computers flash the sell signal. As the orders pour in, the velocity of the decline increases. The process follows one of the basic laws of mechanics: an object in motion tends to remain in motion unless acted on by a superior force. The old "snowball down the hill" allusion. Perhaps the securities industry should supply that superior force. Its attempt to do so, in the form of "circuit breakers," will be discussed later in this chapter.

Index Arbitrage

When the term program trading is used today, it generally refers to a hedging process known as index arbitrage. It combines buy or sell orders in particular stocks with an offsetting position in index futures. No matter which direction is being pursued, the participant will purchase one of the products and sell the other short.

Arbitrage consists of the near simultaneous purchase and sale of the same or exchangeable securities in the hope of making a profit due to a difference in markets. Examples of arbitrage are almost limitless. You might, at a given moment, find it possible to purchase gold at $360 an ounce in London and, at the same time, sell that same ounce at $362 in Zurich. Make the trades quickly, as this discrepancy may not last for long, but if you do so you have a profit of $2 an ounce. A successful arbitrage has taken place.

You may also be able to arbitrage two different securities. For example, XYZ Corporation has outstanding an issue of 8 percent convertible debentures. Each debenture can be exchanged for 20 shares of XYZ common stock. If the bond is trading at par ($1,000), the equivalent value of the stock is $50 a share ($1,000 ÷ 20 shares). Suppose the arbitrageur notes that the bond is trading at 104 ($1,040). She knows that the equivalent value of the stock is $52 ($1,040 ÷ 20 shares), but she sees that the stock is actually trading at $53 a share. She will buy the bond at $1,040 and sell short 20 shares of the stock at $53. The stock sale brings in $1,060 ($53 × 20), resulting in a profit of $20 on the arbitrage.

Program trading can consist of an arbitrage between a futures index, perhaps the S&P 500, and the actual stocks included in the index. While a complete study of this technique is beyond the scope of this book, the basic principle can be stated very simply: if a trader finds a discrepancy between the value of the index and the total value of the underlying securities, and the proper orders are entered, an index arbitrage is made.

Suppose the S&P 500 index future is offered at 380.10. If the multiplier of 500 is used, a value of $190,050 is obtained. At the same time, the stocks that compose the index are trading at prices that total a value of $191,200. Remember, you do not need a pocket calculator to arrive at these numbers. The computer will tell you. It will begin to emit flashing lights and billows of smoke. You buy the index futures and sell the stocks short. You are not even inhibited by the plus tick rule, because it does not apply in this case.

The spread in value shows a $1,150 difference in your favor. While it may not seem like much, understand that the users of these programs are large institutions, banks, pension funds, universities, and corporations. They do not need huge profits on single trades to be successful. If they can improve on the return provided by U.S. Treasury bills, they have done their job. Many dealers engage in index arbitrage for their own accounts. They have an even bigger edge. While a client will have to pay a commission to the broker, the broker does not pay a commission to himself. Though the commission is generally small, perhaps $0.03 or $0.04 a share, it is nonetheless an expense that the broker avoids.

The index arbitrage can work in either direction. If the value of the index future is greater than that of the underlying stocks, you just reverse your positions. You would purchase the stocks and sell the index futures short.

In either case, a cascade of buy or sell orders descends on the New York Stock Exchange trading floor. Prices move up or down sharply, possibly in a matter of minutes. The variation was not instigated by analysis of financial statements, government economic reports, or any other standard measurement of market condition. Charlie the computer made the decision. If he said sell, then the price of your General Motors stock may be driven lower. If Charlie said buy, your short position in Exxon might be in jeopardy. Very rarely does the small investor participate directly in program trading. But he or she is certainly affected.

The Program Trading Controversy

Is an inherent conflict of interest present here? Should a broker recommend the purchase of IBM stock to some clients, while simultaneously selling it short, perhaps for his own account, or as part of an index arbitrage? Again, no answer can be provided. Some major firms continue to engage in this program-trading practice, both on behalf of their clients and for their own accounts. Some state that this market technique has no lasting effect on values, but only seeks to take advantage of temporary situations. This position has resulted in a loss of business for some firms. Clients have refused to place orders with brokers who may, at a given time, be acting for their own accounts, in a manner that is at odds with their clients' interests. Other large brokerage firms compromise the issue by continuing to handle program trades for customers, while abstaining from the practice themselves. Still others, notably Merrill Lynch, will handle no program-trading business at all. As the nation's largest brokerage firm, serving millions of small retail customers, it obviously sees a conflict of interest.

There are two sides to the story, however. Supporters contend that program trading adds to the marketability of securities by increasing the volume of trading. As its effects are generally short-term, it plays no part in the determination of a stock's underlying value. They also point out that computers are the modern method of analysis. If you outlaw the computer as a decision maker, you must also outlaw the automatic transmission in your car and the dishwasher in your kitchen.

Those who would outlaw or severely limit the practice object to its potential to distort the market to such a degree that occurrences far more serious than the market crashes of 1987 or 1989 are guaranteed to occur. One highly regarded money manager has gone so far as to describe program trading as "at best a parasite and at worst a cancer on the stream of useful business activity."

No doubt, program trading has opened up vast new avenues for the short seller. Each arbitrage finds one side to be a short sale. On the other hand, the ability to drive down stock prices without concern for the up tick rule is reminiscent of the pre SEC bear raids of the 1920s and 1930s.

PORTFOLIO INSURANCE

Large brokerage firms that profit from the business of institutional investors have developed systems to reduce the risk of these clients and, therefore, encourage their participation in the market. The strategy involves the use of stock index options and stock index futures. The device, referred to as portfolio insurance, replaced an earlier system that proved to be insufficient to cope with the crash of 1987.

A large institutional client is concerned about the risk involved in its large holdings of common stock. The broker/dealer reduces the risk by selling the client put options on stock indexes. Should the market decline, the institution is protected by its ownership of the index puts. In effect, the risk has been transferred to the broker, who sold short (wrote) the put options. The broker will profit if the market rises, as the puts will not be exercised and the broker will retain the premium received. But should the market decline, the value of the put options will increase and the broker will face a loss. To reduce its own risk, the broker may sell index futures short, which will provide a profit to offset the loss potential of the put options that it wrote. The brokerage firm may also sell stocks as the market declines to protect its position still further.

Since these protective measures become necessary only during periods of market decline, the sales by the broker will exacerbate the fall, causing increased losses to holders of the stocks so affected. Because these holders are often small investors, their position in the market, always risky, becomes further threatened by these machinations of the professional traders. This is just another step forward for computerized program trading. If it is a large backward step in the campaign to encourage public participation in securities, so be it. We cannot place roadblocks on the road to progress. Or can we?

Even the most vocal proponents of program trading admit that the price swings to which it contributes are not good for building confidence in the market on the part of investors. All investments contain some degree of risk, and buyers of securities, large or small, accept that fact. But should the investment process be similar to a blackjack game in Las Vegas, where one can be wiped out at the turn of a card? October 1987 had results nearly this severe for thousands of people.

CIRCUIT BREAKERS AND OTHER CONTROLS

To decrease the volatility of markets, a New York Stock Exchange panel presented a series of recommendations designed to restore the confidence of investors. Principal among the suggestions were requirements that would halt trading in securities if the market rose or fell more than a stated amount within a trading session. These devices, called *circuit breakers,* would remove the immediate stress and allow traders and investors time to regroup. Many variations have been suggested, but most recently the following regulations would apply. If the Dow Jones Industrial Average fell 250 points, trading in stocks would be halted for one hour. The cessation of trading would be extended for an additional two hours following a fall of another 150 points on the same day.

These regulations have not met with unanimous approval. Many feel that they are an admission of the industry's inability to cope with dramatic situations. They argue that investors are not being served by shutting the door to the market in their faces. Perhaps they are correct, but circuit breakers are in place.

Another factor that would reduce the ability of program traders to ply their trade would be to increase the major margin requirements on stock index futures. As stated earlier, professional traders can acquire positions in these contracts by depositing a very small percentage of the value in cash. At this writing, the amount is 5 percent, but has been even lower. Even after the 1987 break, the margin never exceeded 13 percent. On the other hand, purchasers of stocks have a margin requirement of 50 percent, which has been in effect for more than fifteen years. Prior to that time, stock buyers were faced with even higher requirements. In 1945 the requirement was 100 percent. All purchases had to be paid for in full.

Proponents of controls on program trading are actively campaigning for higher margin levels on index futures. This increase would reduce the volume of trading by speculators. Their available dollars would not go as far, since they could not buy or sell short in as large amounts as are now possible. The exchanges on which these contracts are traded, and on which the margins are set, oppose any changes that they do not control. It would be unnatural for them to support any action specifically designed to reduce their business.

Another obstacle to controlling program trading is the SEC's lack of jurisdiction over futures contracts, which are regulated by the Commodity Futures Trading Corporation (CFTC). As the SEC does not have the authority to investigate activities in the futures market, it is unable to detect any improper or fraudulent practices that may employ products from all markets, such as stocks, options, and futures. This situation may change as the regulatory scope of the SEC is increased. Many believe that, before long, futures contracts will be placed under the SEC's watchful eye. This would seem to be a necessary step to arrive at effective regulation procedures. Recently, the chairman of the SEC was quoted as saying: "How can a fire inspector know whether there are too many people in a crowded restaurant if he or she is allowed to look at only half the room?"

It seems likely, then, that program trading will be placed under additional restrictions. Hardly a day passes when it is not a prime topic for the financial pages. It is a strategy in which short selling plays a major role. It toys with the destiny of even the smallest investors. The use of stock index futures grows in importance as new strategies are devised to apply their unique capabilities. They cannot be ignored.

In September 1990 the New York Stock Exchange announced a plan to permit after-hour trading in listed securities. While this development is viewed as the first step toward a 24-hour trading day, it is also designed, in part, as a concession to program trading. Subject to SEC approval, there will be two additional trading sessions, each beginning at 4:15 P.M., fifteen minutes after the close of regular trading. During the first session, which will end at 5:00 P.M., traders will be permitted to enter buy or sell orders into the exchange's computer network. The orders will be matched and the trades will be executed. The second session, which will run until 5:15 P.M., will simplify the execution of program trading transactions. The system will permit the stocks that are included in the index future to be sold at an aggregate price rather than being traded individually. In the completion of these transactions, the plus-tick rule on short sales will be waived.

Only time will reveal the success or failure of this innovation. However, the designation of a portion of a trading session, even if only fifteen minutes, for professional investors to the exclusion of the public is certain to raise many hard questions.

11

Beware the Bear

How should the bear be characterized? Is he the vicious marauder who stalks the woods seeking to crush to death those who would cross his path? Or is he the lovable, public-spirited Yogi Bear who spends weekdays preventing forest fires and Saturday morning entertaining your children, allowing you an extra hour of sleep? It would seem to depend on your point of view. If you are buying stock and a short seller offers shares at a price lower than that at which they would otherwise be available, the bear is your friend. But if he is shorting stocks as part of an index futures arbitrage and forcing down the value of your holdings, he is the predatory beast.

While many examples of the function of selling short have been provided, the total impact on the market cannot be accurately measured. There is no doubt that short sellers greatly increase the liquidity of all securities markets. This is unquestionably a positive contribution. But the bear will also frequently increase the severity of market movements. While short selling can be used to defer taxes and enable arbitrage transactions, in its purest sense it is designed to provide profits due to market declines. It is similar to giving your best friend, who is about to embark on a plane trip to a distant country, a few dollars to take out life insurance at the airport that names you as beneficiary. Success is achieved only at the expense of someone else's tragedy.

Market movements are often caused by the emotional reactions of investors. Short selling is simply a method of expressing one's emotions. When Iraq invaded Kuwait, the markets around the world declined precipitously. In the five weeks from mid-July to late August 1990, the S&P 500 stock index fell from approximately 370 to 308, roughly 17 percent. The fear of economic and physical disaster drove investors to sell securities despite their inability to thoroughly assess this dangerous situation. The rule, as usual, was: When in doubt, sell. No doubt short sellers were also active participants during this period. Even the plus tick rule did not preclude them, opportunities existed each day to sell short. The market did not decline in a straight line, and many rallies accommodated the short seller. Was the short seller taking unfair advantage of an international crisis? No more so than the person who sold securities that he owned. In fact, the "long" seller, uninhibited by the plus tick requirement, was the one responsible for the decline. The short seller cannot force prices down. At most, he can prevent them from going up.

On Wednesday, January 16, 1991, the war in the Persian Gulf began. Americans living in the eastern time zone received the news at about 7 P.M. The financial markets had closed for the day three hours earlier. Although President George Bush had set a January 15 deadline for Iraq to withdraw from Kuwait, most observers were nonetheless surprised by the events of the evening. For the first time in history people around the world were able to watch a war on television. The total effect that this event would have on the future of the planet could not be immediately predicted. But to the investment professional the short-term effect on markets was very obvious. The stock market would suffer a severe decline as it had done when Iraq invaded Kuwait. The threat of destruction in the Mid-East would cause oil prices to soar. The value of the U.S. dollar would rise sharply given the prior history of that currency as a safe haven in times of war. The market professional might have dreamed of the riches he would have accumulated had he known of the outbreak twenty-four hours earlier. He would have sold stocks short, purchased oil futures, and dealt in currencies on both the short and the long side to take advantage of the dollar's certain rise. How fortunate he was that he was not given this vision.

On Thursday, January 17, 1991, the stock market rose 114.60 points as measured by the Dow Jones Industrial Average. More than 318 million shares were traded on the New York Stock Exchange. Most of those who had shorted stocks the previous day were counting their losses. The price of oil lost one-third of its value, declining from $32.00 a barrel at Wednesday's close to $21.44 at closing time on Thursday. Those who purchased oil futures on Wednesday may have been considering a career change. The U.S. dollar suffered a major decline when measured against most other currencies. Those who invested based on the dollar's expected strength were greatly disappointed. ˙ hat happened on Thursday was the opposite of what would have been expected. If there is a lesson to be learned from this, it is not a new one. Markets have always been more susceptible to psychological factors than to rational analysis. Both short sellers and purchasers of securities must constantly remind themselves of this fact. No matter how bright or dark are the economic indicators, it is the optimism or fear of the investing public that will determine the direction of the market. This has been true for centuries. It is obviously not about to change.

There are currently many people who advocate the elimination of short selling. To these individuals it seems immoral to profit from another's loss. But you know differently. All market profits are offset by another's loss. If you purchase XYZ stock at $20 a share and sell it later at $50 a share, you have made 30 points. But what about the poor guy who sold you the stock at $20? Had he not made the sale, the 30-point profit would have been his. Your gain is his loss. Do you try to locate him and at least share the profit with him? Of course not. That's the game. For every winner, there must be a loser. All the short seller does is reverse the usual order of things, by selling first and buying later. In so doing he often helps you, the nonshort seller.

PITY THE BEAR?

Whether you love the bear or hate him, he is deserving of some sympathy. No market participant takes more risk than the short seller. In fact, his risk is often impossible to measure. While he maintains a short position, he is responsible for the cash dividends and other payments that are due to the lender of the stock. He not only has an unlimited risk, but he must often pay for the privilege. Statistics also tell us that for more than one hundred years, the trend of the market has been up, not down. This does not bode well for the bear. While the short seller has had many opportunities to profit, he has been required to move rapidly since the glory moments generally passed quickly.

The Dow Jones Industrial Average can be traced back to 1885. The history of this measurement from the 1929 crash until today reveals the continuing problem faced by the bear. On December 31, 1930, the Dow Jones Industrial Average closed at 164.58. During the summer of 1990, it reached 3000. The market rose in virtually every one of the intervening sixty years, with a few notable exceptions. Relatively severe declines occurred in 1932, 1957, 1970, 1973, 1974, 1978, 1981, and 1984. Even in 1987, the market ended the year at a higher level than that of the prior year. When these declines took place, they were usually short-lived. As they reversed themselves, the short seller is often trapped. So by definition, the bear is not an investor. He is a short-term trader. While you can wait patiently for the stocks you own to improve in value, the bear has no such luxury. You own your stock and have no further financial liability. You may even be cashing dividend checks every three months. The short seller may be called to deposit more margin to maintain his position in rising markets. He is also paying out dividends. If he runs out of money, he must cover his position at a loss. He is often inhibited in his trading by the plus tick rule, which denies him entry to the market at what may be the most opportune moments.

THE SHORT SELLER AND THE 1987 CRASH

An examination of the events during the often-discussed market crash of October 1987 can provide an understanding of the short seller's world. The performance of two stocks over that brief period, IBM and Merck & Co., will be compared for this purpose.

The first signs of the impending disaster were visible on Thursday, October 15, 1987. The decline continued on Friday and Monday, before rallying on Tuesday, October 20. The performance of the Dow Jones Industrial Average and the two selected stocks based on the closing price of each of these four business days is given below:

Date	DJIA	IBM	Merck
Thursday 10/15	− 57.61	140	190
Friday 10/16	− 108.35	134	184
Monday 10/19	− 508.00	103 1/4	151
Tuesday 10/20	+ 102.27	115	154

Between the close on Thursday and the close on Monday, IBM lost about 25 percent of its value and Merck declined 20 percent. There are even more extreme examples. On Monday, October 19, alone, Holiday Corp. lost 37 percent of its value, dropping from 19⅜ to 11⅜ a share. A short seller who accurately predicted these events could have prospered greatly. Even during the trading sessions of Friday and Monday, short sales were possible. Plus ticks occurred during these sessions, giving the bears a chance to play. But even these momentous events lasted only briefly. By Tuesday, October 20, the trend reversed and prices moved sharply higher, assisted, quite probably, by short sellers covering their positions.

It has already been established that market bears are no more intelligent than bulls. They may well have missed this opportunity, just as buyers missed theirs on Monday, October 19. On that day the Dow Jones Industrial Average closed at 1738.74. By the summer of 1990, less than three years later, it reached 3000, an increase of 72.5 percent. Were you in there buying on that Tuesday? Some were, but most, bruised by the events of the three previous days, sat on the sidelines and did not reenter the market. Some have still not returned and, perhaps, never will.

Radical market fluctuations seldom do any good for investors or traders. Both would be more comfortable with orderly conditions, which permit more sober decision making. The professionals who trade for a living may be able to profit on short-term price movements, but most investors tend to be more conservative by nature. But the short seller dines on short-term price swings. His position is not designed for long-term holding. He, in his usual capacity, is not an investor. The bear is a speculator; he could never be mistaken for a conservative. One of the most concise definitions of a conservative is found in Shakespeare's *King Lear*:

> Have more than thou showest
> Speak less than thou knowest
> Lend less than thou owest

A LOOK AHEAD

What will be the role of the bear in the markets of tomorrow? Probably, he will play a larger role than he has to date. While historically the province of professionals, short selling has recently attracted individual investors. A number of market letters are targeted for those investors who seek recommendations from short sales rather than from purchases. Some proponents of the short sale will agree that the market has risen almost continuously, but they point out that this only increases the possibilities for decline. There are even money managers who specialize in placing funds only on the short side of the market, while others are including short positions in portfolios that would not have considered such an approach just a few years ago.

Most newer market strategies use short selling as part of the mechanism. Among them are index arbitrage and program trading. As new strategies develop, the short sale will no doubt be an integral factor.

While short selling has many applications that are not bearish in nature, such as tax deferral and arbitrage, the basic purpose of the device is to make money as a result of declining prices. All legal methods will be utilized to initiate or extend these declines. By no means should short selling be eliminated; it is important to the liquidity of the market. But, as with any market device, it certainly should be carefully regulated to avoid abusive practices. Don't kill the bear. Don't even chain him up. Just watch him carefully.

Although facing the serious problems of unlimited risk, adverse market trends, and continuous costs, the bear is appearing in ever-increasing numbers. He will be exerting pressure on markets, which may compromise the position of other investors. His activities may stifle rising markets and accelerate declining ones. Everyone must be aware of the capabilities of the bear even though you may never join his camp. He is out there, and he is very strong and, at times, menacing. Protect yourself by knowing his history well.

Beware the bear.

Glossary

Glossary

A

advance decline theory See *breadth of the market theory*.

aftermarket The initial market for a security after it has first been offered to the public and before the syndicate is disbanded.

agent The capacity in which a broker acts when he represents a client in a financial transaction and assumes no personal financial risk. The broker charges the client a commission for his services as agent.

aggregate exercise price The total value of an options contract should the contract be exercised. Example: 1 IBM 120 Call would have an aggregate exercise price of $12,000 (100 shares × $120 a share).

arbitrage The near simultaneous purchase and sale of the same or exchangeable security in the hope of showing a profit through a difference in markets.

arbitrageur The person who engages in the market technique known as arbitrage.

assets   An item of value owned by a person or corporation. The left side of a balance sheet lists assets.

at the money   An option contract that occurs if the exercise price of an option and the market price of the underlying security are the same. If XYZ stock is trading at $45 a share and the market price of XYZ is 45, the option is "at the money."

B

balance sheet   A financial report issued by a corporation, listing its assets, liabilities, and net worth.

bear   A person who believes that the market in general, or a stock in particular, will decline in value.

bear raid   A market manipulation in which short sellers force down the price of a stock. They hope to "cover the shorts" at greatly reduced prices.

bid   The price that a buyer is willing to pay for a security or other investment product.

Black Friday   September 24, 1869, the date on which the U.S. government announced its intention to sell gold, causing a panic in financial markets.

Black Monday   October 19, 1987, the date on which the Dow Jones Industrial Average declined 508 points. Volume on the New York Stock Exchange was 604 million shares.

Black Thursday   Thursday, October 24, 1929, the date of the most severe market decline during the crash of 1929.

box   The physical location of securities owned by a firm or a client. (See *short against the box*.)

breadth of the market theory   Also called the advance decline theory. It measures the number of stocks that are advancing in price, declining in price, or remaining stable. Some followers believe it can predict a change in the direction of the market.

broker   A firm or individual acting on behalf of a client and charging a commission for the service. (See *agent*.)

bull   A person who believes that the market in general or a stock in particular will rise in value.

C

call   A contract granting the holder the privilege, but not the obligation, to purchase a specific number of shares of an agreed security at a fixed price for a period of time.

call feature   A provision in a debt security or preferred stock that permits the issuer to repurchase the security.

call loan   A bank loan taken out by a broker, who pledges stocks or bonds as security.

cash trade   A transaction in a security in which delivery and payment occur on the same day as the transaction.

Chicago Board Options Exchange (CBOE)   The largest marketplace in the United States for the trading of options.

Chicago Board of Trade (CBT)   An exchange that provides markets for a wide variety of futures contracts. It is the largest commodity exchange in the United States.

Chicago Mercantile Exchange (CME)   An exchange specializing in the trading of commodity contracts, such as livestock, eggs, and stock indexes.

circuit breakers   A system of controls that requires a halt in trading in securities markets if the market rises or falls a specific amount during a trading session.

commission   The fee paid to a brokerage firm by a client for the broker's services in acting as the client's agent.

commodity   An item of trade that is the subject of a futures contract.

Commodity Exchange Inc. (COMEX)   An exchange that conducts trading futures contracts on precious metals and some nonferrous metals such as copper and aluminum.

Commodity Futures Trading Commission (CFTC)   The federal agency responsible for regulating commodity and futures markets.

corner   A situation in which a person or a group has acquired more shares of a company's stock than are actually outstanding. Those establishing the corner hope to force short sellers to settle their contracts at exorbitant prices.

cushion theory   See *short interest theory.*

customer's agreement   A document signed by a customer opening a margin account, in which the client recognizes the terms under which the account will be operated.

customer loan consent   A document signed by a customer opening a margin account with a broker that permits that customer's securities to be loaned to other parties.

D

debit   The amount of money owed by a client to the broker handling the client's margin account.

Designated Order Turnaround (DOT)   An electronic system developed by the New York Stock Exchange that allows certain orders for stocks to be sent directly to the specialist for rapid execution.

dividend   A payment made by a corporation, usually on a quarterly basis, to owners of that corporation's stock.

Dow Jones Industrial Average (DJIA)   A compilation of the market value of thirty select industrial stocks listed on the New York Stock Exchange. It is the most often quoted measurement of market movement.

E

equity   The portion of a customer's margin account that represents his financial interest in the account. Equity is determined by subtracting the customer's debit balance from the total market value of the securities.

exercise price   The price at which the holder of an options contract can purchase (call) or sell (put) the underlying security.

expiration month The calendar month in which an option contract becomes worthless or in which a futures contract must be completed.

F

Federal Reserve Board The arm of the U.S. government responsible for controlling the supply of money and credit available in the banking system.

fiduciary A person responsible for the reasonable safekeeping of the money or property of some other party. Examples: pension funds, legal guardians, and executors/administrators of wills.

fundamental analysis A method used to determine the value and potential of a corporation's securities that employs analysis of all available financial information.

futures A contract calling for the delivery of a specific amount of the commodity that is the subject of the contract.

H

hypothecation The process of pledging securities to secure the debit balance in a margin account.

I

income statement A report issued periodically by a corporation detailing monies received and disbursed in the course of the corporation's business.

index A compilation of the values of a large group of stocks used to measure the general movement of the market.

index future A futures contract based on the value of a specified market index, such as the Standard & Poors 500. Settlement of the contracts is made in cash rather than by delivery of the underlying securities.

insider   Defined by the Securities Exchange Act of 1934 as an officer, director, or principal stockholder (10 percent) of a corporation. The definition has been extended to include any party that is privy to nonpublic information.

International Monetary Market (IMM)   A Chicago-located market that conducts trading for futures contracts in U.S. Treasury securities and currencies and indexes.

in the money   An option that has an intrinsic value. Example: A call on XYZ with an exercise price of $70 would be 2 points "in the money" if XYZ stock was trading at $72 a share.

intrinsic value   See *in the money*.

J

junk bonds   Debt securities of low investment quality often used to finance mergers and hostile takeovers during the 1980s.

K

Kansas City Board of Trade (KCB)   A market that conducts trading in futures contracts on both wheat and stock indexes (The Value Line Average).

L

lending at a premium   A transaction in which the borrower of stock pays a fee to the lender for the use of the stock.

lending at a rate   A transaction in which the lender of stock pays interest on the money paid to him to secure the loan of the stock.

lending flat   A transaction in which the borrower of stock used to complete a short sale pays no fee to the lender and the lender receives no fee from the borrower.

liabilities   Items that a person or corporation owes and will later be required to pay. Corporate liabilities are listed on the right side of a corporate balance sheet.

limit order   An order specifying the maximum price that a buyer is willing to pay or the lowest price that a seller is willing to accept.

long position   A term indicating ownership of securities. If a person owns 200 shares of American Telephone stock, he is said to be "long 200 Telephone." He is at risk if the security declines in value.

M

margin   The minimum amount that a client is required to deposit when purchasing or selling short securities or other financial products. The requirements, which vary among products, are established by the Federal Reserve, the exchanges, and the individual brokerage firms.

margin call   A notice to a customer demanding the deposit of additional funds or securities due to a change in the value of the client's account.

marketability   The ease with which a particular security can be purchased or sold. It is often referred to as liquidity.

market order   An order to purchase or sell securities at the best price available at the time the order is entered.

market value   The total current value of all securities held in a customer's account.

mark to market   The process of adjusting the value of open contracts. If a lender of stock sees the price of the stock increase by 10 points, he can demand that difference from the borrower.

minus tick   A transaction in a security at a price that is lower than the previous price or lower than the last different price.

multiplier   The factor used to determine the total value of an option or futures contract. The multiplier for the Standard & Poors 500 index future is 500. The current price multiplied by 500 gives the total value.

N

net worth The difference between a person or corporation's assets and liabilities.

new account form A document prepared by a brokerage firm when it opens an account for a new client. It contains all information necessary for determining the suitability of transactions for the customer.

New York Futures Exchange (NYFE) A subsidiary of the New York Stock Exchange that conducts trading in futures contracts on the Exchange's Composite Stock Index and the Commodity Research Bureau Index.

New York Stock Exchange (NYSE) The largest stock exchange in the United States. Founded in 1792, it provides a central marketplace for the securities of approximately 1700 corporations. (As of early 1991 the New York Stock Exchange had returned to the position of largest stock exchange in the world. For a period of time, Tokyo Exchange had claimed the title.)

O

offer The price that a seller is willing to accept for his security or other investment product.

open interest The number of options (or futures) contracts that have been created and have not yet expired or been exercised. Open interest can be measured for individual contracts or for a total market.

option A contract allowing the holder to purchase (call) or sell (put) a specific quantity of an underlying product at a fixed price for a limited period of time.

Options Clearing Corporation (OCC) An organization owned by the exchanges that clears and guarantees all option transactions.

out of the money An option that has no intrinsic value. The option may, however, have a time value.

overallotting A procedure used in new securities offerings in which the manager of the syndicate sells more shares than are actually being offered. The process of repurchasing these shares supports the price of the security in the aftermarket.

over-the-counter The term used to describe transactions in securities that do not take place on a stock exchange.

P

parity The price at which the value of exchangeable securities would be equal. Example: If a bond is convertible into 40 shares of common stock and the bond is trading at 104 ($1040), parity for the common stock would be $26 a share ($1040 ÷ 40).

Philadelphia Stock Exchange The oldest stock exchange in the United States, which provides markets for both stocks and options.

plus tick A transaction in a security at a price that is higher than the previous price or higher than the last different price.

plus tick rule A rule imposed by the Securities & Exchange Commission requiring all short sales made on stock exchanges to be made on a plus tick. It was designed to prevent bear raids.

portfolio The securities and other financial instruments that comprise the holdings of an individual or institutional investor.

Preemptive right A privilege given to holders of common stock to purchase additional shares of that stock, usually at a price lower than the current value.

premium The amount paid by the purchaser of an option to the writer of the contract.

principal The capacity in which a firm acts when it buys securities from or sells securities to a client. The firm assumes financial risk on principal transactions.

program trading A market technique in which common stocks and stock index futures are simultaneously purchased and sold when a disparity in their value is determined by a computer program.

put A contract granting the holder the right to sell a specific number of shares of an agreed security for a period of time.

Q

quotation The highest current bid and the lowest current offering for a particular security.

R

registered representative An employee of a broker-dealer organization who is authorized to service the accounts of clients.

Regulation T A requirement of the Federal Reserve Board that establishes the minimum initial deposit that brokers must require clients to deposit.

resistance level The price level for a stock or market at which sellers historically have been attracted to the market. At this price the security will often decline.

S

SEC Rule 13D A rule requiring the holders of 5 percent or more of the stock of a publicly held company to disclose this fact to the Securities and Exchange Commission. The holder must also disclose his future intentions.

Securities Act of 1933 The federal securities law that regulates the issuance of new securities. Prior to such an offering, prospective investors must be provided with full disclosure of all pertinent information.

Securities Exchange Act of 1934 The principal federal securities law in the United States, which regulates all securities markets in the country and established the Securities and Exchange Commission.

Securities and Exchange Commission (SEC) A U.S. government agency established in 1934 that has total authority to regulate and supervise the securities industry.

Securities Investor Protection Corporation (SIPC) A corporation that insures the brokerage accounts of customers to a maximum amount of $500,000. It was established under the Securities Investors Protection Act of 1970.

share The minimum ownership interest in a corporation.

short against the box The sale of a security that the client owns but does not intend to deliver to the buyer. She will deliver borrowed stock. These transactions are used to defer tax liabilities on capital gains.

short covering The repurchase of a security previously sold short to close out the position.

short exempt Any short sale that is exempt from the up-tick rule. For example, a short sale that is part of a bona fide arbitrage.

short interest theory A theory purporting that a large short position is bullish, as it will provide buyers to support a declining market or accelerate a rising market. Sometimes called the cushion theory.

short position A position in which a client has sold a security that she does not own or does not intend to deliver. If a client sells 100 shares of IBM that she does not own, she is said to be "short 100 IBM." She is at risk if the stock increases in value.

short sale The sale of a security that a client does not own or does not intend to deliver. A short sale creates a short position.

specialist A member of the New York Stock Exchange who is responsible for maintaining an orderly market in a security.

speculator One who is willing to assume large risks in return for the potential for large profits.

spot market The trading in commodities for immediate delivery. Contracts expiring in the current month are considered to be a part of the spot month.

Standard & Poor's Composite Stock Index A weighted index that traces the movement of 500 selected common stocks.

stock parking The illegal practice of transferring ownership of large blocks of stock to a nominal owner to avoid the requirements to disclose such ownership.

stock split   An action in which a corporation increases the amount of stock outstanding without selling new shares. In a 3 for 1 split, the owner of 100 shares would become the owner of 300 shares. The market value and par value are generally reduced inversely.

stop order   A memorandum order stating a price that becomes a market order when that price is reached or surpassed. It is often used to establish or eliminate positions at predetermined prices.

straddle   A trading strategy that includes a put and a call on the same security, each having the same exercise price and the same expiration month.

strike price   See *exercise price.*

support level   The price at which buyers have historically entered the market and purchased securities. This buying activity tends to prevent a decline below this level.

T

technical analysis   An analytical method that employs past price movements and other statistics to predict the future price movements of securities.

tender offer   An offer by a party to purchase all or part of a corporation's outstanding stock at a fixed price.

time value   The portion of an options premium that exceeds the intrinsic value of the contract.

trade   A term used to define a transaction in a security.

trader   One who buys or sells securities for his or her personal account.

U

underlying security   The security or other financial instrument that is the subject of an options contract.

underwriter   An investment banking function in which the brokerage firm guarantees a corporation a price for a new issue of securities. The securities are then offered to the public at a higher price.

W

writer   The party who creates an option contract by assuming the responsibility of buying or selling the underlying security. A writer may be a "covered writer" or an "uncovered writer."

Selected Bibliography

Selected Bibliography

Bernstein, Jake. *How the Futures Markets Work.* New York: New York Institute of Finance, 1989.

Brooks, John. "A Corner in Piggly Wiggly." *New Yorker,* June 6, 1959.

Brooks, John. *Once in Golconda.* New York: W.W. Norton & Co., 1969.

New York Stock Exchange Inc. *A Brief History of the New York Stock Exchange.* 1982.

Pessin, Allan H. *Securities Law Compliance.* New York: Dow, Jones–Irwin, 1990.

Pessin, Allan H., and Ross, Joseph A. *Words of Wall Street.* New York: Dow, Jones–Irwin, 1983.

Pierce, Phyllis. *The Dow Jones Averages 1885–1985.* New York: Dow, Jones–Irwin, 1986.

Securities and Exchange Commission. *50 Years of the U.S. Securities and Exchange Commission.* 1984.

Sobol, Robert. *The New Game on Wall Street.* New York: John Wiley & Sons, 1987.

Teweles, Richard J., and Bradley, Edward S. *The Stock Market.* New York: John Wiley & Sons, 1987.

Index

Index

A

Advance decline theory. *See*
 Breadth of the market
 theory
After-hour trading, 161
Arbitrage, 58–61
 and convertible securities,
 59–60
 examples of, 58–61
 index arbitrage, 147–149
 meaning of, 6, 58, 155–156
 parity, 60
 and preemptive rights, 58–59
 risk arbitrage, 6, 61–62
 short exempt transaction, 60
Assets
 current assets, 121
 fixed assets, 121
 intangible assets, 121

B

Balance sheet
 assets, 121
 capitalization, 123–124
 liabilities, 122
 net worth, 122
 use in technical analysis,
 121–124
 working capital, 122–123
Bear, 9
 characterization of, 163
 and future markets, 168–169
 risk taken by, 165–166
Bear raids, 14, 19
 and corner, 10
 key to success of, 33
 Northern Pacific Railroad, 21–23
 Piggly Wiggly Stores, 11–15
 prohibition of, 33–34
 Stutz Motor Car Company,
 15–19
Black Friday, 24
Boesky, Ivan, 46
Bonds
 bond prices, 112
 short sale, 57–58

Breadth of the market theory,
  125–126
Brokerage account
  cash account, 68
  margin account, 68–70
  new account form, 67–68
  rules for purchase of securi-
    ties, 68–70
Brokers, and short sale, 74–76
Bull, 9

C
Call-loan, 69
Call options, 86, 91–92
  application of, 91–92
  as substitute for short sale, 96
Capital gain, deferral of, 63
Capitalization
  conservation capitalization, 124
  leveraged capitalization, 123
Cash account, 68
Chart patterns, 130–135
  head and shoulders patterns,
    132–134
  M and W patterns, 134–135
  mixed feelings about, 131
  resistance levels, 132
  support levels, 133–134
Chicago Board of Trade, 137, 142
Chicago Mercantile Exchange,
  138, 144, 147
Circuit breakers, program trad-
  ing, 159
Combinations, 100–102
Commodity, meaning of, 137
Commodity Exchange, New
  York, 142
Commodity Exchange Inc., 138
Commodity Futures Trading
  Corporation, 160
Computers. See Program trading

Conservation capitalization, 124
Convertible securities, and arbi-
  trage, 59–60
Corner, 10, 14
Covering the short, 3
Crash of 1929, 25–27
Crash of 1987
  events of, 167
  and short sale, 166–169
Crashes, and program
  trading, 155
Current assets, 121
Current liabilities, 122
Cushion theory, 127
Customer's agreement, 70–71
Customer's loan consent, 70

D
Designated order turnaround, 154
Douglas, William O., 30, 31
Dow Jones Industrial Average,
  history of, 166
Drexel Burnham Lambert, 47, 49

E
Equity options, 86–96
  call options, 86, 91–92
  nature of, 86–91
  put options, 86, 92–93
Ethical considerations, short
  sale, 3–5
European currency units, 108
Exchange rates, 107
Exercise price, 87
Expiration months, futures con-
  tracts, 139

F
Federal Reserve Board, 68
Federal Trade Commission, 28
Fees, and short sale, 80–81

Finders, 75–76
Fixed assets, 121
Floor brokerage, 54
Foreign currency contracts, futures market, 141, 144–145
Foreign currency options, 106–111
premiums, 108, 109
and risk, 111
shorting of, 109
trading process, 108–109
uses of, 109, 111
Full Disclosure Law, 27–28
Fundamental analysis, 115, 119–125
balance sheet, use of, 121–123
income statement, use of, 124–125
Future, meaning of, 137
Futures contracts, 137–140
expiration months, 139
foreign currency contracts, 141, 144–145
hedging, 142–146
increase in participation in, 146
limits on price fluctuations, 124–125
margin account, 129–130
open interest, 129
options contracts, compared to, 138–139
prices, expression of, 139
short sale, 140–142
on stock indexes, 138
trading exchanges, 137–138
types of commodities, 138

G

Gold, and Jay Gould, 24–25
Gould, Jay, 24–25
Great Depression, 14, 21
Crash of 1929, 25–27

H

Harriman, E. H., 22–23
Head and shoulders patterns, chart patterns, 132–134
Healy, Robert, 28
Hemline hypothesis, 117
Hill, James J., 22–23
Hypermarkets, 11
Hypothocation, 69–70

I

Income statement, use in technical analysis, 123–124
Index
nature of, 147–148
stock index futures, 148–152
Index arbitrage, 155–157
Index option, 103–106
nature of, 103
premium, 103
and Standard and Poor's 100 stock index, 103–104, 106
trading process, 104–105
uses of, 106
In the money, 89
Insider trading, 39–45
insider, definition of, 39
outside "insiders," 43–45
regulations related to, 39–43
Insider Trading Law of 1988, 43
Intangible assets, 121
Interest rate options, 111–113
uses of, 112
Interest rates, and Treasury securities, 112
International Monetary Market, 144

J

Junk bonds, 46–47

K

Kansas City Board of Trade, 138
Kennedy Joseph P., 28–30, 31

L

Landis, James, 28, 31
Lending at a rate, 80
Leverage, pros and cons of, 123
Leveraged capitalization, 123
Liabilities
  current liabilities, 122
  long-term liabilities, 122
Limit orders, 84
Livermore, Jesse L., 12–13
Long sale, 38
  meaning of, 2–3
Long straddle, 97, 99
Long-term liabilities, 122

M

M and W patterns, chart patterns, 134–135
Margin account, 68–70, 93–94
  documents signed by client, 70
  futures contracts, 145–146
  rules for purchase of securities, 68–70
  stock index futures, 149
Margin call, 70
Market analysis
  chart patterns, 130–135
  fundamental analysis, 115, 120–125
  hemline hypothesis, 117
  index futures as substitute for, 151–152
  random walk theory, 116–117
  Super Bowl Theory, 117–120
  technical analysis, 115, 125–130
Market orders, 83–84
Mark to market, 77

Matthews, George, 28
McChesney Martin, William, Jr., 30
Milken, Michael, 46
Morgan, J. P., 22, 29–30
Municipal Securities Rulemaking Board, 28

N

National Association of Securities Dealers,
  creation of, 28
Net worth, 122
New issues, short sale, 64–65
Northern Pacific Railroad, 21–23

O

Open interest, futures contracts, 145
Options
  equity options, 86–93
  Options Clearing Corporation, 88–89
  premiums, setting of, 89–91
  and short sale, 88
  as substitute for short sale, 93–96
Orders
  limit orders, 84
  market orders, 83–84
  stop orders, 83–86
Out of the money, 90
Outside influences, and investing, 51

P

Parity, 60
Pecora, Ferdinand, 27, 28, 31
Persian Gulf war, 165–166
Philadelphia Stock Exchange, 108, 110

Piggly Wiggly Stores, 11–15
Plus tick rule, 34, 38
Preemptive rights, and arbitrage, 58–59
Premium, 59, 80, 87–88
  foreign currency options, 108, 109
  index option, 105
  for options, 89–91
  straddles, 97–98
Program trading, 152–158
  circuit breakers, 159
  controversy related to, 157–158
  and crashes, 155
  designated order turnaround, 154
  index arbitrage, 155–157
  portfolio insurance, 158–159
  process of, 153–155
  regulations related to, 159–161
Proxy, 79
Put option, 86, 92–93
  application of, 92–93

R

Random walk theory, 116–117
Regulation T, 68–69, 70–71
Regulation U, 69
Resistance levels, chart patterns, 132
Retirement strategies, 63–64
Rights and obligations, short sales, 76–79
Risk
  and bear, 165–166
  and foreign currency options, 111
  and investing, 51
  and short against the box, 63
  and short sale, 51–52

and short sales, 78
and straddles, 99, 100, 101
Risk arbitrage, 6, 61–62
  example of, 61
Risk minimization and short sale
  combinations, 102
  equity options, 86–96
  foreign currency options, 106–111
  index options, 103–106
  interest rate options, 111–113
  stop orders, 83–86
  straddles, 96–100
Roosevelt, Franklin D., 28–29
Rumor spreading, about value of stock, 38
Ryan, Allan A., 15–19

S

Saunders, Clarence, 11–15
Securities Act Amendment of 1975, 28
Securities Act of 1933, 27–28
Securities Exchange Act of 1934, 27, 33
Securities and Exchange Commission, 160
  creation of, 28–30
  reform of stock exchanges, 30–31
Securities Investor Protection Corporation, 81
Short against the box, 62–64
  examples of, 62–64
  meaning of, 6
  reasons for use, 62, 63–64
  and risk, 63
Short exempt
  meaning of, 7
  transaction in, 60

Short interest theory, 127–130
Short sale
  arbitrage, 6, 58–61
  benefits to market, 5–7
  bonds, 57–58
  and brokers, 74–76
  effects on brokerage firms,
    75–76
  as emotional reaction, 164
  ethical considerations, 3–5
  to facilitate other transactions,
    52–57
  fees related to, 80–81
  futures contracts, 140–142
  future view, 168–169
  historical importance of, 7
  inadvertent involvement in, 81
  and insiders, 42–43, 44
  margin account, 68–70
  meaning of, 1–2
  new issues, 64–65
  and 1987 crash, 149–151
  options as substitute for, 93–96
  process in, 70–74
  rights and obligations, 76–79
  and risk, 51–52, 78
  and risk arbitrage, 61–62
  risk minimization, 83–113
  short against the box, 6, 62–64
  short exempt, 7
  and specialists, 57
  speculation by selling short,
    49–52
  and tender offer, 44
  transaction in, 34–39
Short straddle, 97, 99
Specialists
  as agents, 53–57
  book of, 54–55
  as principles, 56–57

  role of, 34, 53–57
  and short sale, 57
Speculation, by selling short,
  49–52
Standard and Poor's 100 Stock
  Index, 103–104, 106
Standard and Poor's 500 Stock
  Index, 137, 147, 148
Stock indexes, futures contracts, 138
Stock index futures
  applications for, 149–152
  determining value of, 148
  and institutional investor,
    149–152
  margin account, 149
  as substitute for market analy-
    sis, 151–152
Stock parking, 45–47
  illegality of, 46–47
  process in, 45–46
Stock splits, 83–86
  meaning of, 84
  problem related to, 85–86
  stop limit order, 86
  uses of, 84–86
Straddles, 96–100
  long straddles, 97, 99
  nature of, 96–97
  premiums, 97–98
  and risk, 99, 100, 101
  short straddle, 97, 99
Strike, 87
Strike price, 102
Stutz Motor Car Company,
  15–19
Subscription price, 58–59
Super Bowl Theory, 117–120
Support levels, chart patterns,
  131–132

T

Technical analysis, 115, 125–130
  breadth of the market theory,
    125–126
  short interest theory, 127
Tender offer, 43–45
  process in, 43
  rules related to, 44
Trading post, 34
Treasury securities
  calls on, 112
  and interest rates, 112

U

Underlying stock, 87

W

Whitney, Richard, 30–31
Working capital, 108–109

Z

Zero-plus tick, 37–38